The PARADOX of CRE

Wake Up You Are
God In Disguise

Published by ProduktFokus
© 2013 Camillo Loken

First Printing: April, 2013

<u>Cover</u>
Idea: Camillo Loken
Graphics: NUVO Creative Studio, www.nuvostudio.com

Second Edition: July, 2014

ISBN 978-1484157947

www.TheParadoxOfCreation.com
www.WakeUpURGod.com

This book is dedicated to

You

- The Creator of All –

The One Mind

Seeking manifestation for its
Potential in the finite realm

You truly are God in Disguise.

Table of Content

FOREWORD

Is our world an illusion - a hologram? Leonard Susskind is a professor of Physics at Stanford University and he is known for given a precise string-theory interpretation to a theory by the name of The Holographic Principle. Several physicists like Professor Peter L. Galison, Professor Brian Green, Professor Leonard Susskind and others say that this theory explains how our universe might actually be a gigantic hologram - an illusion. The entire Universe might just be the 3D projection of information found on a 2D information structure at the edge of the Universe. [1.1]

If this is true who or what created this hologram? God? Many people in the scientific community have trouble just hearing the word God. Why? Because the word God is often related to religion as a generic term for various belief systems that assumes that reality encompasses more than the physical. And it is hard to accept for scientists who rely on evidence and proof to validate our reality. In general we only believe what we can see - seeing is believing. The physical world is what we relate to. To speak of an invisible God as a creator seems too far out for many people. It definitely was too far out for me. For many years I was an atheist and a skeptic. Why? Because I grew up in a family of physicians and atheists. I believed life on Earth to be the result of a cosmic coincidence and when we die we are gone forever. This view was modified during my teens, but my true passion for the spiritual started with an awakening in 2006. An obsession to find answers to who we are came over me, where we come from, what we are doing here and where we go when we die? I became a spiritual seeker looking for a bridge between science and spirituality - to see the connection between the

4

two. My quest led me to answers showing me this bridge and this totally changed my life. I left a secure job in the pharmaceutical industry to embark on a journey leading me to incredible meetings with psychics, channelers, shamans and people with near-death experiences from many different continents. During my exciting journey I was also invited to have a special meeting with the renowned humanitarian, spiritual leader and ambassadors of peace Sri Sri Ravi Shankar. Meeting these people provided me with more pieces to the puzzle in finding out who we really are and why we are here. However, I never stopped searching and I often ask the Universe for help in understanding more about creation. One day yet another piece of the puzzle came into my life. An e-mail from a person who has had the experience of being as close to the core of creation as possible found its way to my inbox. The e-mail was from Steve Berg in the UK. What he shared with me impressed me. What he later on revealed about creation resonated with me and expanded my consciousness. He has been a great contributor to the content of this book providing me with incredible insight and knowledge about creation.

I know now that it was my destiny to meet these people and I was supposed to write books, host seminars and do talks about creation and the ongoing shift in consciousness. It was all part of the character I play in this lifetime. I was supposed to grow up as an atheist and then end up working in one of the biggest international companies in the pharmaceutical industry only to leave it all behind - to become a spiritual seeker. I had to see and experience opposite views of creation in order to gain a broader understanding of it - both ends of the scale so to speak. I am still occupied with finding out more about creation, where we come from, who we are and what we are doing here. During the last few years many people have also become increasingly preoccupied with these questions. Why? Is it all part of a Divine Plan or is it just a coincidence? I do believe it's part of a grander Plan and a cycle we move along in order to re-member more about who we really are.

Since my awakening I have spent almost every hour of the day thinking about creation, and who we are and why we are here. This is my true passion. I have found answers resonating with me, but by no means do these answers represent *the one and only truth*. The content of this book is as such based on my research, my truth and my perception of reality. In short I provide an overview of the cycle of creation as I have come to know it. For some readers the content of this book will feel right - the information will resonate with them. Others will be provoked by the same content and call it lies, fantasy and just nonsense, maybe even blasphemy. Even though people don't see eye to eye on issues regarding life and creation I do believe it's important to keep an open mind no matter how "radical" another point of view might be. A closed mind is like a closed book - just a piece of wood. An open mind does not judge. *Observation is power - judgment is weakness.*

I always refer to the wisdom of Buddha before I speak at lectures or seminars. I also want to refer to his wisdom in this book. However, I am not a Buddhist. I do not belong to any specific religion, but his words contain great wisdom beyond the boundaries of any religion:

Do not believe in anything simply because you have heard it. Do not believe in traditions because they have been handed down for many generations. Do not believe anything because it is spoken and rumored by many. Do not believe in anything because it is written in your religious books. Do not believe in anything merely on the authority of your teachers and elders. But after observation and analysis, when you find that anything agrees with reason and is conducive to the good and the benefit of one and all, then accept it and live up to it.
- Buddha (563 – 483 BC)

How do you know if something *agrees with reason and is conducive to the good and the benefit of one and all?* You know it when you use your intellect *and* your heart. Most people are quick to judge others if their values and truths are not matching their own. They judge others based on their ego - based on their intellect. They never connect with the heart and allow for a broader view - a more open minded view of reality. If they did they might be able to see through the eyes of another. If more people connect with their heart and with their intuition this world will change for the better. Connecting with the heart is letting the Yin energy, the feminine energy, rise and balance out the dominating masculine Yang energy. I do believe the balancing of the Yin and Yang energies are in progress. More people connect with their heart and get in touch with their intuition. It´s all part of an ongoing shift in consciousness. This shift is part of a huge cycle of creation from forgetting to re-membering. It is the Divine Plan. All is Mind and we are it. We are points of consciousness representing this One Mind and it is using the physical world - the space-time construct - our Universe - to create and experience in order to be. This One Mind is God wanting to define and know Himself. It´s all about *being by doing.*

ACKNOWLEDGEMENTS

We sleep so we can wake up and the time of awakening is now. My awakening came from the insight and wisdom of the people I met, the eye opening books I read and the spiritual movies I watched. They helped me wake up from a sound sleep where I was living my life on autopilot. As such I want to express my deepest thanks to all those who contributed to my awakening. A big thank you to John O'Leary who helped out editing the book. I am truly grateful for your time and effort. Also, a special thank you to my good friend Steve Berg from the UK, a person I consider to have great spiritual insight. Thank you for your knowledge, expertise, wisdom, attitude and insight as to the reason we all exist. Thank you for sharing your incredible experience of being in the core of creation and providing me with valuable eye-opening information for this book. It has been a pleasure to exchange ideas and thoughts about life and the reason we all exist. We have been sharing the same truth, our truth. You have been able to provoke thought in me, as I have in you and this must continue. I would also like to express a special thank you to my wife Synnøve, our children and my parents for the support, help and understanding you have given me since I chose to embark on this journey - a journey to find answers to who we really are and what life is all about.

INTRODUCTION

This book came about as a result of my meeting with Steve Berg in the UK. He got in touch with me through my website One Mind One Energy (www.one-mind-one-energy.com). Steve told me about his amazing experience many years ago where he had an incredible expansion of consciousness. He was guided and shown how the cycles of creation are driven by the core paradox of the infinite and the finite - how everything is One Cosmic Mind. This mind is both infinite and finite at the same time. It's like being asleep and awake in the same moment. It is an impossibility. It's a paradox. Here is an excerpt of what Steve explained to me about the paradox of creation:

Everything already 'is.' The finite, and in that the linear existence, is an experience of what eternity is, and eternity is not a very long time anymore than infinity is a very big 'thing.' Eternity actually means no time, no time passing. We exist, "now". No one exists in the past or future, we only exist now. The appearance/experience of past and future are achieved by exploding the "now". Like that the infinite is a movie that is complete, an is-ness, but then you can't know the movie that way. You have to watch it frame by frame. Pass the frames across the lens in sequence and it seems to be moving. The infinite does not move, it 'is'. There is no void of unknown future to move into - to allow for movement, no next moment, there is no other than the infinite. The infinite is not divided into dark and light, apparent and void, all is ONE and so it is still and unobserved. The infinite 'is'and it is on one static "now". That's why you can't be aware of it, because awareness is a feedback loop, re-cognition, and that requires time, past present and future for the feedback! Again it's why you sleep and wake, your mind as a fractal copy of the ALL paradoxically reverberates from each contradicting state, chicken, egg, chicken, egg. The paradox never resolves. So you are awake/aware, with a sense of space-time in mind, and then

you sleep with no re-cognition facility. The Sleep peelS as you wake. The
infinite explodes to create a void to move into. This is the Big Bang.

The universe was un-manifested before the Big Bang. A potential. An infinite mind which has the potential to be anything. It is something abstract. Some scientists say that the universe came out of nothing, but there is no action in nothing. Nothing remains *"nothing."* It cannot turn into *"something."* When we talk about creation nothing means No Thing. It is not a thing, yet. It is not concrete, solid. It is infinite potential that has the ability to become something - anything. The Big Bang can be seen as the beginning of the transformation from nothing to something. The un-manifested becomes manifested. The abstract becomes concrete, and for this to happen there must be intelligent design behind all creation - a creator - a God. God realizes its potential by creating a space-time structure - a place/an environment where it can create, do and experience the un-manifested. Creation is all about manifesting the un-manifested. The potential is being realized. The infinite mind wants to realize itself. It wants to love itself because there is only one mind. Alone. Many spiritual teachers say that we are all one, but being one is being alone. Look at the words we are All One. All One is the same as Alone. ALL ONE = ALONE. It's a code. This mind must therefore create a game to *not* be alone. It wants to bring forth love, which unfortunately also evokes fear to define this love. As such we experience the world of duality as part of this game.

The paradox is that the cosmic mind is both unconscious and conscious at the same time. The mind has infinite, un-manifested potential (unconscious - like a sleep state) and at the same time it 'creates'a finite world, The Big Bang where it is conscious (awake) and able to experience. The Big Bang moment is like smashing a puzzle into billions of pieces. Then the pieces are slowly but surely put together as complete picture. Logic is the tool we use to understand creation. We use logic to find new pieces of the puzzle and put them together. When the last piece of the puzzle has been found the cosmic mind has gone full circle in the finite world. So what happens next? The finite and the infinite 'meet/intersect' at Steve calls this The Paradox Point - the core. This is the point where you can no longer be conscious. The finite world has reached its end. It is the exactly same thing each and everyone of us does each night when we fall asleep. We are conscious, and slowly but surely we move into a unconscious state and fall asleep. The point where our conscious state is left behind and where we move into an unconscious state is the paradox point.

The Law of Correspondence is a universal law and it states that what happens on the macro level also happens on the micro level. As above so below. So we do what the cosmic mind is doing, we experience the paradox point but it happens so fast we cannot be aware of it. When the cosmic mind reaches this point there is nothing more to experience in the finite world. There are no more pieces left in the puzzle and therefore everything must start again. A new Big Bang. The puzzle is being smashed once again and spilt into billions of pieces only to be reassembled all over again. It is like watching a movie and when it´s finished it restarts. In chapter none I will go into detail about the paradox of creation and I will also talk about creation including intelligent design. But if science is right then the Big Bang came out of nothing without the intervention of a divine being. How can that be? How can creation come from nothing and at the same time involve a divine being - an intelligent entity? Science sticks to no divine creator, but religions across the world beg to differ. They claim God, an intelligent entity, created the world. Who is right? *Both are right*, but how is that possible? We´ll get back to that, but first Who is God? What is God? A quick internet search on the word God will give you millions of hits. The word God is probably one of the most known words in the English language. We are conscious beings and we all have a concept of God. In other words, in consciousness you have a concept of God, but is there a God prior to the word God? The word God and the concept of God is a superimposition that consciousness puts on the absolute prior to words. We need consciousness to have a concept of God and as conscious beings we often see God as the Creator of all of Creation - a supernatural creator who is omnipresence (in all places at the same time) omniscient (has infinite knowledge), omnipotent (has unlimited power) and omnibenevolent (is all good). The interpretation of God has evolved from how the early philosophers interpreted, to how current religions and people from all walks of life are defining God today. Who is this mysterious God? Is God All That Is and All That Is Not? Is God All and Nothing? If so, how can anyone or anything be nothing? We'll get back to that too.

It seems like everyone has some meaning or definition of what God is or is not, but there really is not any objective definition for the term. No definitions of God are adequate because to define God is to limit God. God goes beyond the boundaries of human comprehension - it goes beyond the boundary of logic and science - it goes beyond consciousness. God is more than science and more than logic. God is also Magic - the unseen - the un-manifested - the infinite. Some people will say God is a force outside our selves, but others disagree. They say God is a force within. Yet some also say that God doesn't exist at all. Who is right? Below is a list of these three categories of people and their views of God.

1. People who believe in God as an EXTERNAL force

These people believe in a God as an EXTERNAL almighty force - a force outside ourselves. A force that we need to worship and pray to for help. The All Seeing God that dwells in Heaven.

2. People who do NOT BELIEVE God exists

These people do not believe in any God force. God is non-existent. These people rely on science, and science alone. Matter is all that matters. Many just laugh at the idea that some unseen God Force created this Universe and is omnipresence. They believe everything to be a result of a cosmic coincidence and they are using logic to find the answer to the origin of creation. Some say it all came out of nothing. Others keep looking and searching for more answers. They want hard solid proof so they stick to what science can prove. We don't need a God to make the Big Bang go bang, they say.

3. People who believe in God as a force WITHIN

This third category believe that the God force is real, but it´s not an external force. It´s a force we are a part of. It´s within each and everyone of us. It´s saturating everything - every atom in the physical world, the finite world and it´s also in the unseen - the un-manifested infinite. This God is ALL MIND. This God is All and Nothing - this God is within you.

God cannot be found outside you, because there is no God who can ever be outside you. Godliness is the ultimate fragrance of your consciousness.
Osho

This third and last category of people do not believe God to be an external God who is supposed to be an overseer of humans and the Universe. These people believe that **we are** the GOD force and we are part of All That Is. This resonates with me. I do believe we are like cells in a body - individual cells, but together the cells make up the body. Together we are God. We are part of a Cosmic Mind - The Mind of God. Nothing external. All Is Mind and we are part of that Mind. We are the ones in control of creation IF we understand that our thoughts and feelings are the forces that run the Universe.

We create the so-called heaven and hell, because we are God in Disguise. We are the architects and the dreamers of the great matrix of expression and creation.

We are God, but we are hiding from ourselves in order to gain as much as possible out of the experience of expression. Why? It´s part of the set-up to know who we really are - for God to know who God is. What we experience is the potential of God. God is all knowing, but not all experienced. God has the potential to be or do anything, but until God lives out that potential it will forever stay a potential. As such we are created as soul aspects to manifest the potential - the knowing - of God. In creating and experiencing we become the mirror, the reflection needed for God (ourselves) to really know Himself both as a potential and as an experience.

Alberto Villoldo has gone through two near-death experiences and he explains why you are here:

Within infinity you became the architect and the dreamer of the great matrix of expression and creation. So you are here to express and create and if you don´t do that you are caught in someone else's dream - someone else's nightmare. The practice of Infinity is really about dreaming your world into being. [1]

Being God in Disguise sounds farfetched if you are an atheist relying on science. I should know because I used to be one. I grew up in a family of physicians. It was a family of atheists and academics - a very scientific environment. To me life on Earth was the result of a cosmic coincidence and there was no such thing as life after death. God was not present in my upbringing, but in school they talked about Jesus, God and the Bible, it made no sense. I had been told God did not exist so I didn´t "buy into it". Just a fairytale!

When we grow up our brainwaves are in the lower areas - theta and delta. From age zero to six there is no conscious filter. As such we are being molded and formed by the ones responsible for our upbringing. They are our primary teachers. So, as a child I was conditioned to believe that creation was a cosmic coincidence and when we die we are gone forever. I modified this view during my teens, but it wasn't until many years later that I experienced an awakening and became passionately interested in finding answers to four BIG questions in life:

1. Who we are?
2. Where do we come from?
3. What are we doing here?
4. Where are we going when we die?

Over the years I have devoured many books giving me answers to these four questions. I also acquired much knowledge from meditation, various courses, channeled sources, webinars and films, and by talking and discussing these topics with shamans, mediums, people with near-death experiences, and with other open-minded people. This quest for answers resulted in my first book *The Shift in Consciousness* (*www.TheShiftInConsciousness.com*) - a book bridging science and spirituality. The book contains references to scientific material showing us that we are thinking beings, living in a thinking universe, and we possess tremendous powers of creation within ourselves. We are here to discover that we are the Source - God - that expresses and manifests Himself through the uniqueness possessed by each and everyone of us. You are unique. Your thoughts are like mental fingerprints. No one can think or feel exactly like you do. Why is that? Why are we all unique? It's part of The Plan - part of the construct set up by The Mind - God - in order to experience His vast potential in the finite world - in the physical plane through as many individuals consciousness' as possible. You are a part of this Plan and you are unique. You are a point of consciousness in The Mind of God. We all are. When you understand that you really are the Source that expresses itself through your uniqueness, you understand that you also possess the most fantastic powers of creation. You have the ability to think independently of circumstances and as such you can create everything your heart desires within this space-time construct which is like an illusion, but a great one at that. It's a hologram - something current science is now beginning to understand. Their mathematical formulas and equations show that our Universe most likely is a gigantic hologram. They call their theory The Holographic Principle - where a hologram encodes 3D information on a 2D surface. The entire Universe might just be the 3D projection of information found on a 2D information structure at the edge of the Universe. But can there really be an edge to the universe? No. Why? We'll get into that too, later on in this book.

The Holographic Principle holds that the information which describes all of the particles of matter and vibrations of energy in the bulk of the sphere fundamentally "lives" at the boundary of the sphere. It's like the Universe is a consciousness hologram where reality is a projected illusion within the hologram. It is a grid system created by The Mind for the purpose of experiencing creation. We perceive it as our reality - a reality used as a "doing environment" for The Mind. Reality is really thought construction. *The core substance of the cosmos is consciousness.* Thought is an attribute of consciousness, the filter through which consciousness manifests itself into the hologram of form. This illusion is so real and it has to be otherwise the set-up will not work. We would be onto the illusion and not gain as much from this experience as we do now. This illusion is like a movie and you are starring in it. You play a character - we all do, but it's a character. It is not who you really are.

There is no person, it's all a concept, it's all an illusion. [2]
Sri Nisargadatta Maharaj

Even though The Holographic Principle is just a theory and as such not an established truth, I am convinced that the Universe is a hologram. Mediums have been channeling information about this hologram for decades. I read a lot of channeled information and I have seen how science is arriving at conclusions about creation which are coinciding with previous channeled messages. I do believe that channeled information play an important part in helping people see the bigger picture of creation. And that is why my first book *The Shift in Consciousness* also included several such messages. However, since the publication of this book in 2011 my understanding of creation has grown even further. A need to share this new information and understanding with fellow souls became apparent, resulting in this book you are now reading. One of the key points in this book is that you are God in Disguise and that you are here to manifest the un-manifested - to create and do in order to be. This and some other key points will be mentioned several times throughout this book. Why? Because repeating something over and over again will lock it into our subconscious mind and ultimately change our vibration and what we attract into our lives. These key points will help you become a conscious co-creator.

The power of creation - God - is within all of us. Why? Because All is Mind. Yes, you are part of this Mind - this consciousness - you are God in Disguise and now it´s time to wake up to this reality so you can move on to the next level in this creation game. You need to increase your vibrations and raise your level of consciousness. This will lead you into new dimensions, new levels where you can partake in new ways to create and experience - still all in The One Cosmic Mind.

Is this the truth? Are we really consciousness? Are we God in Disguise? Who can claim they know the whole truth about creation? No-one since truth is dynamic. I am merely stating my point of view and I am asking you as a reader to keep an open mind. My truth might not be in harmony with your truth and that´s perfectly OK as long as we don´t judge each other. An open mind is what is driving the understanding of creation. History has shown us that the truth is always changing because our understanding is changing.

CHAPTER ONE

TRUTH - BEING A RED DOT

In 2011, I published my book <u>The Shift in Consciousness</u>. The book set out to answer 4 big questions in life: Who are we? Where do we come from? What are we doing here? Where are we going? I used many different sources to arrive at answers providing me with a sense of peace and understanding. I found answers showing me a bridge between science and spirituality, and an intelligent design behind creation - a universal consciousness - a Source - a God. These answers work for me - they resonate with me, but they do not represent a universal truth.

The truth can never fully be known, because the whole creation is a paradox not allowing for a finite solution to its great creation. So, is there a God - an intelligent design behind all of creation? Is God real? Is God an Almighty force - the Creator of all? Is this true? Or is the whole creation a result of a random expansion starting with the Big Bang? A bang that came out of nothing as stated by some scientists. Did energy just appear out of the vacuum app. 13.7 billion years ago turning itself into matter to then evolve into this incredible Universe we now live in? Is this the truth? Yes, some part of science will tell you that this is the truth, but others disagree. The different religions in this world stick to God being the Creator. Who is right? What is the truth?

WHAT IS TRUTH?

Most people ponder this question at some time in their lives. This is especially true when they are struggling with the question of the meaning of life. The need for meaning is a basic human need, and there can be no meaning without some ultimate truth. This truth has as such been a topic of discussion in its own right for thousands of years, but can there be an answer to this question? A logical mind would say it cannot be answered because there is no truth; how can you answer it? On the other hand, the truth is so vast, it is not definable. The truth is so huge, enormous; it cannot be reduced to language. It is forever changing and can never be static.

As such, the so-called established truth keeps changing as we progress in our understanding of creation. This is what history has shown us. The Earth used to be flat, but it wasn´t. It was round. Then it was believed to be the center of the Universe until Nicolaus Copernicus and later Galileo Galilei pointed out that this was not the case. Galileo supported the work of Copernicus who claimed that the Earth was not in the center of the Universe.

When in 1633 Galileo stated that the sun was at the center and that our Earth orbited the sun he was put on trial by The Roman Catholic Church. He was 70 years old and was accused of heresy. Galileo was convicted, but due to his old age the sentence was altered to house arrest in his home in Arcetri, Florence for the rest of his life. He died in 1642. He opposed the Roman Catholic Church, scholars and the masses, and was convicted for his views, but today he is hailed as the father of astronomy. Galileo and Copernicus were right and the Roman Catholic Church and the others were wrong.

One would expect such an historical event and others like it to change mans' narrow mindedness - to help us become more open minded. Sadly - this is not the case. We still judge other people because they hold a different view of the world and of reality than we hold ourselves. History has been kind to us since it has provided plenty of opportunities for us to learn and see that being open minded is the way to be. By now we should have grasped the idea that judgment is a weakness and observation is a strength. Sadly we keep a closed mind and ridicule anyone daring to challenge the so-called truth. However, truth is dynamic and never static.

So, who is dictating the truth? Throughout history we have had *two truth providers - religion and science*. For a long time religion was truth provider number one, but was later replaced by science who is now running 'the truth show.' Today truth is dictated by what can be measured and proven, but even though you can't see or measure certain things it doesn't mean it's not there. Before the invention of the microscope bacteria did exist, but since they can't be seen with the naked eye no-one really knew they were there. Along came the invention of the microscope and presto - we could see them - we discovered bacteria.

What is proven to be true is tied to what we have available as measuring and seeing devices. This, of course, changes as we progress in the field of technology. Today we are much more advanced with regards to technology than we were 100 years ago, but still new technologies will emerge. In the future a new picture of reality will be established - probably much different from the current view.

Absence of evidence is not evidence of absence.
- Carl Sagan

We like to keep the truth boxed up so we can relate to it. We have a frame of knowledge and within this frame is the so-called truth. People challenging this "box of truth" are being labeled crazy or out of their minds if they cannot back up their views of reality with hard solid evidence. Let me give you an example. If I told you that UFOs are for real and that the Universe is filled with different life forms you might burst into laughter and say:

No way. Are you out of your mind? There is no such thing as aliens and UFOs. It's all science fiction. Anyone saying UFOs are for real is just plain crazy.

Another point of view might be:

Yes, of course. I have seen several UFOs and even been in contact with aliens.

Who is right and can claim the truth? The first version or the second one or both? The first one would ask for proof - convincing proof, but in truth such a person would probably need to have a UFO experience to believe it to be true since no evidence would ever be good enough. The second version claims to have seen UFOs and even talked to aliens. In fact this might very well be a person who used to be a skeptic, but due to personal experience changed his or her truth about UFOs.

The truth is that UFOs and aliens are just science fiction for some and real for others. It's all about the persons own experience and his/her perception of reality. Maybe the so-called disclosure would see the light of day and all the newspapers and TV stations and heads of governments would come clean and say:

Yes, UFOs are real and they have been around since 1947, but we have been hiding the truth from you.

Even then many people would be in denial and doubt. Why? Because most people need to see to believe. It's not enough to just hear about it. And hear about it you can. Here 's how: from April 29th to May 4th in 2013 The Citizen Hearing on Disclosure was held in the National Press Club in Washington, DC. It set out to accomplish what the U. S. Congress had failed to do for forty-five years - seek out the facts surrounding the most important issue of this or any other time - evidence pointing toward an extraterrestrial presence engaging the human race. Hearing witnesses testified for 30 hours over five days. Witnesses included some of the top researchers in the world along with government/agency/ political persons of rank and station. One of them was former Defense Minister and Deputy Prime Minister of Canada, the Hon. Paul Hellyer and he said this:

"...but just as some children survive the idea of tooth fairy, and Santa Claus when they become adult, I think that taxpaying citizens are quite capable of accepting the new and broader reality that we live in a cosmos teeming with life of various sorts. The fact that some civilizations are more advanced than ours, may be humbling, but that could be a necessary step in our survival."

He also said this about technology of clean energy:

"It exists and it is being kept secret by the same vested interests that control our destiny. Who are these vested interests and what are they up to? Well, Senator, you were talking about a military junta. In my opinion that is true, but I have broadened and deepened the definition to Cabal, and the Cabal comprises members of the three sisters. The Council on Foreign Relations, The Bilderbergers, and The Tri-Lateral Commission, The International Banking Cartel, The Oil Cartel, members of various Intelligence organizations, and select members of the military junta, who together, have become a shadow government of not only the United States, but of much of the Western World." [60]

As is often the case, the world media under-reported this

game-changing event. Most people have not heard about this hearing because mainstream media never picked it up. However, if people do hear about it they are not going to believe what the different hearing witnesses shared. Why? Because they want more proof. They want to see this information being covered in the mainstream media and last, but not least they need *to see* in order to believe. They will never believe in any alien life form and the cover-ups just because someone like Paul Hellyer says it is true.

We are brought up to verify everything through our five senses and seeing is the sense that provides us with the most extensive information about the outside world. 'Seeing is believing' is what most people live by. If you can see it, then it is real. If you can´t, it doesn´t exist. You can´t see bacteria, but they exist all over your body. You can´t see mites, but they too are part of the physical world. They have always existed even before the invention of the microscope, but back then no-one knew about this "invisible world". How could they? Bacteria and mites can´t be seen with the naked eye. Today we know they exist because we can see them through a microscope.

Imagine if you went back in time to the era before the invention of the microscope. Imagine you decided to tell people about bacteria - these tiny "creatures" crawling all over our bodies. What would happen? How would people react? Most likely they would have labeled you a complete nutcase - as someone who had lost it. Why? Because it could not be proven. On the other hand, if you brought with you a microscope they would be able to see these tiny "creatures" up close. They would probably declare you a genius for discovering this "invisible world".

Galileo was ridiculed and sent to jail for his beliefs, but when science and people caught up with his genius, he was already dead. He was recognized and hailed as the father of astronomy after his death. Galileo was ahead of his own time and helped the world excel and move forward. He was a *red dot*. Are you like Galileo? Are you a red dot?

WHAT IS A RED DOT?

Imagine a huge black frame. It´s the frame of knowledge based on science and current established facts. Within this frame is the so-called truth. It´s being kept inside the frame. It ´s like a box of truth. The frame is made up of tiny, black dots defending its content. These dots keep the frame intact, but who are they? They are people who need to see in order to believe. Their only truth is the truth inside the frame. They stick to it and defend it. You find these black dots everywhere. They are your neighbors, your colleagues, your friends and even your family members. These black dots are the masses who only believe in the so-called established truth. They stick to what science can measure and what science says is true.

The frame can only change when someone challenges it, but who is brave enough to do that when the result might be embarrassment and ridicule or even imprisonment as in the case of Galileo? What happens when someone starts to question the frame and its content? What happens when someone starts to question the established truth? They move out of the frame and away from the common belief of the masses. They don´t conform. What then? Immediately they become *a red dot* standing outside the black frame for all to see. The black dots are shocked. Someone is questioning the truth. Someone is crazy enough to be outside the frame and not comply with what we know - with what science is telling us is true. They do not *conform*. How stupid. Have they lost it? They can´t prove what they are saying so they must be out of their minds.

To be a red dot requires courage and boldness because the community of black dots making up the black frame of "truth" is massive. They defend the "truth" and want people to stay within the frame. They scream:

Get back in here - don´t challenge the truth, because we know the real truth. It´s inside the frame. There is nothing out there. Rely on science to tell us what is true. Let them measure and prove our reality to us. CONFORM. CONFORM.

Red dots provoke, challenge and sometimes confront the black frame. They are indeed brave red dots existing outside the frame and as such they are helping the world and humanity progress and evolve. We need to challenge the truth of creation because the truth will always change. Why? Because we are part of an ongoing cycle to re-member, and the truth provider called science is limited by our current technology, what can be measured. Science uses logic to explain creation; however, logic alone cannot explain it. Creation is more than logic - it´s also *magic* - there´s a mystical part we cannot see or touch. The mystery of The Cosmic Mind.

Science is looking for proof and evidence before something can be established as true, but absence of evidence is not evidence of absence. Even though we can´t see something it´s not the same as non-existent. There is more to this world than meets the eye. Yes, some people will agree. Maybe they have seen a UFO when others did not. What then? Most likely ridicule. The masses will probably call them crazy. According to the black frame of 'truth'UFOs don´t exist. They will say it´s all imagined and explain it as seeing weather balloons or airplanes.

The masses will not keep an open mind because they are

blinded by the black frame and its "truth". It's the only truth they know. Another example: Let's say you saw a ghost. To you it was real, very real. What would happen if you shared your story with others? Most likely ridicule and being labeled crazy. The masses would try to drag you inside the black frame. *Get back in here. We know the truth. Ghosts don't exist. You probably just saw the curtain moving.* You would answer: *No - I saw something dark passing me and I could even feel it.* And the masses would reply: *You are imagining it - it was probably just your own shadow.* Very few people will keep an open mind when a red dot challenges the black frame and the so-called "truth".

Let's say someone had a near-death experience and saw the Light. They went to the Light. They met deceased loved ones and experienced the God Force. To them this experience was as real as life on Earth. They were conscious, they felt, saw and experienced another reality as real as this one. When they "came back" they decided to share their story. What would happen? Most likely people would not believe them. A typical reaction might be: *Your brain played a trick on you. It's not real. It's just in your imagination.* Who can blame them for such a reaction? Most people have not had a near-death experience. They stick to what they know and to what science has proven to be true. Anything outside the frame is farfetched. Here is another farfetched example. Imagine you told people that trees and plants can pick up our thoughts. They would for sure label you a complete nutcase and say:

Trees and plants are just that - trees and plants. They can't "pick up" anything.

The black dots in the frame would all laugh in your face and call you crazy. This idea would be so foreign from their so-called established truth and there is no-way they would believe you. You would need to prove it to them and still it would be so far reaching that even more proof would be required. Well, Clive Backster has proven this very thing through 40 years of research and still people don´t believe it. Why? Because the masses - the black dots - are not ready to take in such a truth. It´s too far out there. His research is called bio-communication (primary perception) and you can read more about it here: http://www.one-mind-one-energy.com/biocommunication.html.

Our history is filled with brave red dots challenging the black frame of established truths. Unfortunately many of them were ridiculed, jailed or even burnt at the stake. Others were able to prove they were right and then hailed as geniuses.

In our modern world we think we are open minded, but many are not. We think we know it all, because we are modern, sophisticated people on top of the food chain with great technology at our fingertips. We think we are so smart, but still we judge and criticize people because they challenge our precious frame of truth. This frame is really rigid and hard to break out from. It takes a great deal of courage to do just that.

It´s even harder if you are all by yourself and no-one supports your view. As soon as you have someone to share it with, someone who believes in you, it becomes easier to stick to your own truth and not give in to what the masses say about you and your truth. Too many people have ended up in psychiatric hospitals as crazy people because they were brave enough to tell other people what they experienced or saw, but unfortunately, as long as the experience is outside the black frame of established truth it doesn´t fly. They will look at you as a red dot - someone not conforming to the established truth. They can´t allow that so they try to "box you in".

REDS DOTS - THANK YOU

If you are a red dot I salute you. I am proud of you, because you are helping the world progress and not stagnate. And you should be proud of yourself. History has shown that red dots challenging the so-called truth are the ones helping us evolve further. People like Galileo. We need red dots. God and creation need red dots because they help people understand more. In fact they help us re-member who we are step by step. They are re-minding us. They are necessary characters playing out their part on the great cycle of creation from "forgetting" to "remembering."

Another historical event showing how red dots help move the world forward involves the discovery of radio waves. Guglielmo Marconi was an Italian inventor. He introduced the world to radio communication, but no-one believed him. No-one thought it was possible to transmit signals through the air without wires or cables. His colleagues and other scientists wanted to institutionalize him. They thought he was mad. On June 2, 1896, Marconi applied for a British wireless telegraphy patent. Shortly afterwards he also applied for and was granted a US patent. He knew it was possible to transmit wireless signals through the air, even though all the experts in the world said it could not be done.

He proved them wrong! Marconi was granted the honor of inventing the radio, but it´s worth mentioning that Nicola Tesla was the first one to patent the wireless transmission of radio signals. He demanded that Marconi's patent should be invalidated. He claimed Marconi had used his technology and several months after his death in 1943, Tesla was finally recognized as the father of radio.

Tesla, Marconi and Galileo were all red dots channeling the so-called truth. When science through new technology finally catches up with the red dots the frame of "truth" expands and includes them. Instead of being ridiculed they are hailed as geniuses. Nevertheless, when the new truth eventually is established another red dot will appear and challenge that new truth.

Why? Because the truth can never be boxed in. It is too vast to be held and explained by any frame or box. The human race knows very little about the incredible creation we are part of. Cosmologists looking into the vastness of the Universe keep saying that the more they discover about the Universe the more they realize how little they actually know. No-one knows what this physical world really contains and no-one knows what the un-seen world contains. As such the "frame of truth" will always expand.

All is Mind - and as such all is possible. If you can think it, it can be real - as real as The Mind lets it be. Scientists are discussing the existence of many universes - multiverse - and they say they are like bubbles on top of each other. Also, several physicists like Brian Green (Prof. Colombia University) and Leonard Susskind (Prof. Theoretical Physics. Stanford University) are saying that we might very well be living in a hologram - that the entire world we see is an illusion. They talk about The Holographic Principle.

This really stirs things up among the black dots holding the black frame of "truth" in place. Even though physicists are able to use math and formulas to show the likelihood of our world being an illusion the black frame will not change immediately. Why? Because the black frame is made up of people (black dots) defending the current, established truth with all their energy.

It takes a very long time and a lot of convincing evidence to admit a new truth. Even though someone has in fact proven the current truth to be wrong and that a new truth must take its place it will not be accepted straight away. It takes time to sink in as in the example of the flying machine.

When the Wright Brothers invented the flying machine and were air born for the first time only a handful of people witnessed it. Seven years passed before the average American believed flying to be possible. They finally believed it when they saw a picture of President Roosevelt sitting in an airplane. Being a red dot is cumbersome and hard work, because the black dots are constantly trying to pull you back into their black frame of "truth".

First they ignore you, then they laugh at you, then they fight you, then you win.
- Mahatma Gandhi

A red dot is often ridiculed and labeled crazy, but if you are a red dot and you believe in your view of the world stick with it. Don´t let the black dots scare you or intimidate you to give up on your "red dot status". You wouldn´t get an idea or a different viewpoint if you didn´t have the courage and power to stick with it. It´s part of the character you play. Just by resonating with an idea proves you have the strength within you to hold on to that idea. It´s like Wallace D. Wattles wrote in *The Science of Getting Rich*:

Doing what you want to do is life; and there is no real satisfaction in living if we are compelled to be forever doing something which we do not like to do, and can never do what we want to do. And it is certain that you can do what you want to do; the desire to do it is proof that you have within you the power which can do it. [3]

This is also true for what you want to believe in. Don´t let the black frame tell you what is true and what is not. Creation is too grand for anyone to claim to know the whole truth. Listen to your inner voice and feeling and you will find the truth. This is the intuition that many of us have neglected and ignored. Why? Because we are told to only rely on our five senses. As such we are letting the external world tell us what is "true". All we need is a time-out in our hectic day and *go within* to get in touch with the inner voice and feeling. It gives us the guidance we need to understand more of this great creation. It is The Cosmic Mind talking to us as Neal Donal Walsch explains in his book *Conversation with God*:

God: My common form of communication is through feeling. Feeling is the language of the soul.....I also communicate with thought....I also use the vehicle of experience and finally when feelings , thoughts and experience all fail I use words. [4]

Most people will only stick to their five senses and with the so-called "current truth". It´s easier and more comfortable. No-one will ridicule them for conforming with the established truth. It´s safe to agree with the masses, but who has the authority to say that the only version of the truth is their own version? Is it science? - because they can prove the current view? The current view is only valid until new technology measures a different world and gives us a new truth.

When we grow up we are being presented with what is true. We are being told what is right and what is wrong. Those in charge of our upbringing do their best to give us their picture of the world and as such we are being conditioned from the day we are born. Our primary "teachers" are our parents, siblings and the local community. However in many cases they are the "black dots. They conform and follow the masses. As such many of us are being molded and sculpted into black dots. Soon we have a set of values and our own "truth" which is equivalent to the "established truth". As we get older we might adjust our view of the world. However the core values and truths we grew up with are part of our thinking patterns locked inside our subconscious mind. They will stay there until the day we decide to reprogram our beliefs and our "truth" - until the day we challenge the "established truth".

Many people are lost in their own "truth" - a truth they inherited from their parents and the society they grew up in - "the established truth". Think of this: what you consider to be true today would probably not be true if you had grown up with parents not conforming to the current, established view of reality.

Throughout history religion as a truth provider has used its powers to influence people to believe in their version of the truth - in their version of God and creation. Like sheep in flocks we have followed and believed religious leaders and their messages of creation and of God. These leaders have acted as intermediates between the people and God. As a result they have gained great power and influence. Throughout history they have claimed to hold the truth about God and creation, and we have let them. Are they all telling the "truth"? No, the true spiritual message has been totally corrupted by these religious leaders so that they could perpetuate the status quo of their wide and ranging vested interests. P.M.H Atwater puts it like this in her book *We Live Forever - The Real Truth About Death:*

No religious teaching practiced today survives intact from its original source. Only chosen texts and approved interpretations remain for our use.[5]

No one and no religion can honestly claim to know the whole and absolute truth about life and all its secrets. Everything simply IS because All is Mind.

As human beings we decide whether something is right or wrong, true or false. Our ideas about right or wrong change with time. As an example, burning people at the stake was an accepted punishment for men and women accused of heresy or witchcraft in the 16th and 17th centuries.

It was 'right' because it was believed to cleanse the souls of those accused. Today this form of punishment is considered wrong. The 'right' changed to 'wrong.' We also see different 'rights and wrongs' in different cultures, religions and places. What is right for some is wrong for someone else. Your experience of the truth might be perceived as being completely wrong when seen from a different perspective. Hence, what you experience as truth is true for you, but it might not be true for someone else, it´s not a universal truth.

It´s different perceptions of what we call reality. All is Mind and The Mind is experiencing itself within a hologram - an illusion - our space-time construct where everything is energy and everything is vibrating at its own specific frequency. When people tune into the same frequency they see and experience the same truth. As in the previous example with the UFO - one can see the UFO and the other cannot. Why? Because of frequencies. The one who sees is tuned into the same frequency as the UFO.

All is Mind and we experience different "parts" of this Mind based on what we tune into. This explains why some can talk to dead people, some see ghosts, some see UFOs, some see the future, some do remote viewing, some see auras etc. It´s all about frequencies and what we tune into. As such it is important to always keep an *open mind*. A closed mind is like a closed book - just a piece of wood. We need to open the book in order to see what it contains and if the content is not in harmony with what we believe to be true it's OK. However, we should refrain ourselves from judging those who appreciate and resonate with the same content. In other words, when you meet people with a different version of the truth than your own *observe - don't judge*.

My truth is that we are God in Disguise. We are cells in a cosmic body. All the cells make up the body and 'the body' is God. Our human body consists of billions of cells and they need to work together in order for our body to function and be healthy. The cells have different tasks and jobs and when they perform their tasks the body is healthy and fine. On the other hand, when they forget who they are they can attack each other. When this happens our body gets sick and we end up with autoimmune deceases. When cells malfunction the body breaks down.

We are soul aspects of The One Mind. We are points of consciousness and through us The One Mind creates and experiences. As Gary R. Renard also mention in *The Disappearance of the Universe:*

The Mind has seemingly split itself up so that each unit observes the dream from a different point of view, which explains your own personal experiences. [5.1]

This means that some souls/points of consciousness will experience what we label 'bad'and others will experience what we label 'good.' We are all connected and when 'bad things' happen it affects the global consciousness field. In other words it affects us all since we are all one. All is Mind and The Mind uses the different points of consciousness (us) to create and experience who it is.

As souls using a human body we have forgotten who we are and we end up attacking each other. We have forgotten our mission which is to express the potential of God - to experience and live out the potential through our own uniqueness. We had to forget in order to do this. Forgetting is part of the set-up, but not on a permanent basis. We are supposed to re-member and those who re-member must re-mind the others. Sadly we have been forgetting for a long time. We hurt and caused pain and suffering to each other. As humans we think we are separated and not connected when we in fact are All One. It´s time to move along the cycle. It´s time to re-member. More and more red dots are helping us wake up and expand our consciousness and our perception of reality.

The way forward is by unity and co-operation instead of separation and competition. More people are waking up to the fact that we are all connected like cells in a body or points of consciousness in The Cosmic Mind. No matter what gender, skin color, sexual orientation, religious stance or view point on reality we are all equally important representations of The One Mind playing our character in the movie called Life. The Mind is experiencing the manifestation of its infinite, un-manifested potential of consciousness through each and everyone of us in the finite realm. The Mind wants to feel how it is to go from an abstract state to a concrete physical one. It wants to feel how it is to be physical and dense instead of just "floating consciousness" - an un-manifested thought - a potential.

The Mind has to forget its own truth in order to be part of "reality". It has to tie itself to a linear time frame or the experience won't stick. It creates a 'bubble' of time and space (which we call the Big Bang) in order to experience its vast potential. It needs to create a mirror to really see and know itself. The infinite un-manifested potential of consciousness seeks the finite and that is in itself a *paradox*. The infinite is like the sleeping part of the cosmic mind and the finite is waked part. The cosmic mind is both asleep and awake and that is impossibility - a paradox. The infinite is still. No movement. It's like a static now. It just is. There is no space of unknown future to move into allowing for movement. In order to be conscious and alert it must create a void to move into - a bubble of space and time - a Big Bang that turned into this incredible universe we see today.

The universe is just like a game with certain rules. The rules are the universal laws. These laws are the basic rules for the game we call reality, the parameters of the program. The cosmic mind must set it all up in order to go from a state of infinite and un-manifested potential to a state of tangible, physical and limited experience. One of these universal laws is called the law of vibration. It sets in motion the law of attraction which is a secondary law since it rests on the law of vibration. In this game everything vibrates. Everything has its own frequency. The game of life is therefore a game of frequencies.

CHAPTER TWO

THE FREQUENCY GAME

If you want to find the secrets of the Universe, think in terms of energy, frequency and vibration.
Nikola Tesla

Some people are awake and they are now re-minding others that we are God experiencing the God potential. We start to realize that *matter is NOT all that matters*. Some part of science is discovering that all is consciousness - all is Mind and this Mind has created a construct of space and time with universal laws as real as the Law of Gravitation in order for us to play the game of frequencies.

A construct of space and time is needed to do, to create and to experience. Our Universe is that construct and Earth is part of it. It´s a 'playground'- a doing environment needed to live out the God potential - to create, to do, to experience in order *to be*. The construct also contains universal laws making up the "rules of the game". By understanding these laws we become conscious co-creators and realize that nothing happens by chance. There are no co-incidences. We create them ourselves with what we think and feel which sets up The Law of Vibration which triggers The Law of Attraction drawing what we want to experience into our lives.

Within this space-time construct we call reality everything has its own unique frequency something the great inventor, engineer, physicist, and futurist Nikola Tesla (1856 – 1943) discovered. It led him to many great inventions. In order for us to find the secrets of the Universe, he said, we must think in terms of *energy, frequency and vibration.*

Yes, this is true, but we can´t see the vibrations. We can´t see the ocean of energy we live in. We can´t see other peoples auras or other energy fields, but there are people who can. Why? Because they are tuning into these frequencies. How? By lowering their brain waves. When we lower our brain waves from beta to alpha we allow for awareness beyond our normal active waking state and are able to be more sensible to surrounding energies. When you shut down external stimuli and turn your mind inward and focus on self-reflection your brainwaves shift moving from beta to alpha and then further down to theta. The ego loses its grip on you and the soul awareness arises. Some people do this with ease; others need to meditate for a long time in order to lower their brain waves. Still others never mediate and never see or feel the surrounding energies. Since most people can´t see these energies they don´t believe we live in an ocean of energy so they dismiss it.

Since birth we have been relying on our five senses to verify if something is real or not. Seeing is believing and if we can´t see it (measure it, prove it) - it doesn´t exist, but we do not see with our eyes. We see with our brain. All our five senses are sending electrical impulses to the brain and the brain is interpreting these signals. Why? It´s part of the construct set up by The Mind. We are playing the game of life and we must think it´s real otherwise the game would not be believable. If it's not real, then reflectively, neither are we. To make it work we need some great tools to facilitate a reality that we think is real. God is hiding from Himself and if the reality we observe and live in was less real we would be onto the set-up and the construct. However, it´s orchestrated is such a great and clever way fooling us to think that the reality we observe through our five senses is real - very real.

Of course the finite realm has to look as logical as possible. Otherwise we would see through it. When we arrive as soul aspects within the space-time construct to gain experiences - to live out the unlimited, un-manifested potential, we are like babies, but then we learn and grow (which is actually to re-member). As such the construct has to be complex and conform to the laws of physics for the best part at least, and yes when we see through the illusion, then that creates a whole new game.

As human beings we can´t comprehend that our lives are illusions - that we exist inside a hologram, but this is what science is telling us now through The Holographic Principle. The math and the formulas used by physicists support the idea that we might very well be living inside a hologram. It´s mind blowing and incredible difficult to grasp. It´s beyond human comprehension. Our reality is so real and we don´t realize it´s all a game - that all is Mind - that we 'live inside'a Cosmic Mind - The Mind of God. Since we can´t see this Mind we dismiss it. We call it nonsense. It can´t be true. As humans we tend to rely on what we can measure and prove. We need to see in order to believe.

OUR FIVE SENSES

From the day we are born we see and feel through the physical body and in that are naturally conditioned to believe that the world we live in is an absolute material reality. We grow up under the effect of this conditioning. We let our five senses tell us what is real. We build our entire life on the viewpoint that the world is one of matter. However science has discovered that reality is not one of matter, but one of frequencies and energy.

Our five senses act like antennas picking up information about the external world. The world we know of consist of what our eyes sees, what our ears hear, what our noses smell, what our tongues taste and what our hands feel. These five senses are our tools and we are dependent on them from the day we are born. They are at our disposal and they lay the foundation for how we perceive the world. We only know the external world in the way it is presented to us by these five senses. However, scientific research has revealed a different picture altogether of the world we see. Our senses tell us that the external world is solid. You see a table and you can touch it. It feels real and solid. However, it only appears solid to our senses. Science is showing that the table is actually energy vibrating at a certain speed. It has its own unique frequency. This is also true of everything else we believe to be solid. In other words matter is not matter. Albert Einstein realized that matter is actually energy:

Concerning matter, we have been all wrong. What we have called matter is energy, whose vibration has been so lowered as to be perceptible to the senses. There is no matter.
- Albert Einstein

Others have also touched upon this - one of them was Napoleon Hill. With the help of industrialist Andrew Carnegie, one of the world's richest men of his time, the author Napoleon Hill spent two decades interviewing hundreds of successful people. They were well-known for their wealth and achievements. Their collective wisdom was collated in a book entitled, *Think & Grow Rich*, published in 1937. In his book Hill also talks about how matter began as an intangible form of energy:

This Earth, everyone of the billions of individual cells of your body, and every atom of matter, began as an intangible form of energy. Desire is thought impulse. Thought impulses are forms of energy. [19]

Everything is combinations of energy. This gives an illusion of form, something solid. Our five senses perceive everything around us as being solid and separate because everything is vibrating at a speed that makes it look solid. All objects are constantly vibrating at their own frequency— the book you are reading now, your sofa, your mobile phone, your car, even your whole self. You are broadcasting frequencies all the time.

Everything is energy, but our five senses are fooling us to believe that the external world is solid. If I smash my hand onto a table I can feel it, I can heard the sound it makes and I can see it. It is so real and solid, but still it is energy and nothing but energy. When we take this one step further we discover that All is Mind. Our world is an illusion, but how can it be when it´s so 'real?' It´s hard to grasp since we trust our five senses to tell us what the real deal is. However, if you sit on a beach and gaze out on the ocean it looks like the ocean blends and melts with the sky in the far horizon. We know that´s not the case, but this is what our eyes see. The same with railroad tracks. If you look down a rail road track it looks like the tracks are crossing each other further down the track. We know it is not true, but this too is what our eyes see.

Any good magician can easily perform tricks making us see and experience something which is not true. They can make things 'disappear.' We know it´s a trick, but still it looks real. Creation itself is a magic trick. God is the greatest magician of all and God is running the reality show because there is only One of us here.

In terms of the physical you can feel pain from a lost limb, this because signals are still being sent down the remnant of the severed nerve, you can feel the pain in a limb that is not there! This because reality is nothing more than a set of signals interpreted by the brain, experienced within the psyche. All you really need is the signals, the information, in order to create a sense of reality. And the mind can do that itself as seen in dreaming. So a greater mind controlling a collective reality? It's certainly feasible even to a skeptic, indeed in dreams your mind creates 'others»! The One Cosmic Mind called God is creating the reality. As God says to Neal Donald Walsch in *Conversations with God:*

Every event is an Act of God. Do you imagine that an event could take place if I did not want it to? Do you think that you could so much as lift your little finger if I chose for you not to? [4]

We are all God in Disguise and as such God through us is running the show. God needs a doing environment in order to run the show - in order to create and experience. Our Universe is such a place. We think it is real, but it's not. It's a hologram - an illusion. A great illusion - the greatest trick ever. Some people are now realizing that it is in fact a 'magical trick», an illusion in order for God to experience Himself - to seek manifestation for all its potential. We are all God in Disguise playing this thought game. However, the majority of people on Earth are still being mesmerized by this magical illusion and think it's real. Yes, it is incredible real. All our five senses keep verifying that the world outside ourselves is real.

You can see a flower, touch it, smell it and it's real. Yes, real in this wonderful world which is actually a hologram - a construct for us to experience ourselves. As such we should enjoy every minute of the time we spend on this beautiful Earth. The Earth is a brilliant destination, a hidden diamond that is about to reveal its true beauty because we are about to create Heaven on Earth.

When you realize that the Earth and everything on Earth is part of a grand illusion in the bigger Divine Plan and that you are God in Disguise your time here will be even better. Why? Because you know we are here to enjoy this beautiful planet and the manifestation process from idea to realization - to appreciate life in every moment.

Most people take life for granted not realizing how the space-time construct is in place as a tool to help us enjoy creation. They think the world is real and random. And then the pacifying view of an impossible religious eternal heaven subconsciously makes people look forward, and in that disrespect the now. When this is gone it's gone! We only exist once! Every time around is the first and last time for all intents and purposes. What would their heaven even be? What would you do to keep busy and happy for the first few billion years?

Noting that a few billion years won't even scratch the surface of forever! Many people see the external world as real and random missing the bigger picture. The world seems to real. When you look out into the Universe and see the stars far away from planet Earth you are in fact "seeing" the stars inside your head. We don´t see with our eyes, but with the center of vision in the brain. This is the construct. It´s part of the illusion.

THE ACT OF SEEING

Our eyes provide us with the most extensive information about the outside world. We see the external world as a place of matter, but it´s not as science is showing us. Our eyes deceive us. At the instant of seeing light particles or photons travel from the object to the eye. They then pass through the eye lens where they are refracted and focused on the retina at the back of the eye. Then the information is passed on further as electrical signals by neurons to the center of vision at the back of the brain.

The act of seeing actually takes place in the center of

vision in the brain. Everything we see and experience takes place in this center of vision which is just a few cubic cm. The center is inside a dark brain sealed from light. So we see and observe a colorful and bright world inside our dark brain. When we say we see we actually observe the electrical signals in our brain. As such every single atom, every single tree, every single star and planet and the entire Universe is not really matter, but electrical signals in our brain. When you see your body you think that you are inside of it. However your body too is an image formed inside your brain.

Try telling this to a person who has never heard of how the eyes send electrical signals to the vision center allowing us to see. Immediately you will labeled as a red dot because you challenge the so-called 'truth.' The masses don´t know this. It ´s not a known fact. People think they see with their eyes, peeping out of a hole in your head? But you are not 'in there.' The soul that animates the body can never be found in the physical. They think what they see is real. It is not. It is electrical signals being turned into images inside our brain - in our vision center. We actually see with our mind and that is why people with NDE can see when the go to 'the other side.'

The truth is that when you are apparently awake during the day and you have your eyes open, it´s not really the body´s eyes you are seeing with anymore than when you´re asleep at night. It is always your mind that is seeing. It´s always your mind that is hearing and feeling and doing the other things you give the body´s senses credit for. There is no exception to this. The body itself is just part of your projection. From the book The Disappearance of the Universe by Gary R. Renard. [5.1]

Our current view of reality would have been regarding as pure science fiction 100 years ago. What we know today about the act of seeing, about energy, stars and planets, the human body and the incredible machinery within our cells was unthinkable only a century ago. Not possible - not real. Why? Because it could not be measured, proven and seen. Take the cell for instance. Today we know how complex it is. Biochemist Michael Behe, author of *Darwin's Black Box*, points out that:

The simplest self-replicating cell has the capacity to produce thousands of different proteins and other molecules, at different times and under variable conditions. Synthesis, repair, communication - all of these functions take place in virtually every cell. [20]

If we go back to Darwin's time, they thought the cells were little more than tiny blobs of gel. Most scientists at that time speculated that the deeper they delved into the cell, the more simplicity they would find, but the opposite happened. Little did they know that the future would see the invention of electron microscopes and advanced research techniques revealing an incredible level of complexity in each cell. It´s just mind blowing. If you travelled back in time and explained what a cell contained to people in the times of Darwin you would certainly be a red dot outside the black frame and you would be ridiculed for your statements.

As human beings we live by our five senses and we judge others who are not able to prove their version of reality with hard, solid evidence. If we can´t see it and measure it - it can´t be real. However, history has shown how the masses and the so-called experts have been wrong on many occasions. Even though we can´t measure or see something it doesn´t mean it is non-existent. When looking at creation we should be more modest and open minded.

Judgment is a weakness - Observation is a strength.

Everything is energy. Everything you see and touch in the physical world is vibrating on its own specific frequency which again is part of The Mind since All is Mind. The Mind was here first. Everything else kicks in in order for The Mind to define and experience itself, and experience is linear, so we keep on rolling along in the space-time construct of energy.

We basically live in a sea of energy and we are surrounded by frequencies (energies). Even though we cannot perceive these frequencies with our five senses, they do have an effect on us like the life energy known as qi or chi in China and as prana in Sanskrit. Life energy exists inside us, through us and around us, but then on a slight shift of perspective, it's not energy per se, energy suggests something tangible, we are mind! We are a paradigm in motion.

The world that you are familiar with, the physical, material world, is not the only one in which you move and interact. Every day when you get up, shower and go to work, each and every step reverberates through two sides of reality at once. Your physical body walks in the world of matter, but a subtler aspect of you, woven within and throughout your physical body, moves and interacts on a level of pure energy. - Michelle Belanger [21]

Yes, everything is energy and these energies surround us, just like radio waves and cell phone waves surround us. There is so much invisible movement and information being broadcasted and transmitted all the time from radios, cell phones, TV, WiFi towers, satellite dishes and more. Information! Data! That's what creates reality, likened to the programming that underlies the appearance of an animated image on a pc screen. You can see the whole thing as a series of ones and nothings 01010101, energy being the description we use for values of information.

These energies float around as particles and waves and they all have a particular vibration. They are subject to a Universal Law called The Law of Vibration. This law is as real as the Law of Gravity. Both Laws are part of the construct that makes up this space-time reality. Everything vibrates. The same with human beings. We all have a particular vibration. A personal frequency - our own, special vibration which we radiate out.

In her book *Frequency - the Power of Personal Vibration* Penny Peirce talks about a personal vibration and a home vibration. The home vibration is the vibration of your soul - the essence of who you are. Your personal vibration is the frequency of energy you hold moment by moment in your body, emotions and mind. You set this up yourself with what you think and feel.[22]

Most people let the external world influence them and as such it will affect their level of personal vibration. As an example - watching negative news will influence your thinking and your feelings and as such change your personal vibration. The more we let the outside world influence us the more we give away our power to control what we are vibrating out into the ether.

We must stand guard at the gateway to our minds. We must be conscious of what we let inside of us. All the water in the world cannot drown you if it doesn't get inside of you, but if it does you die. Letting negative information from the external world 'get inside of you'will affect your life. If you let the external world and the negative news and violence get into your mind it will affect your vibration. Negative information will cause a low and slow vibration and whatever you send out will get back into your life. Maybe not right away, but it will return.

This is the Law of Cause and Effect which is another law in the construct. It's part of the set-up so we can play the game of life. The Universal Laws governing our lives are the 'playing rules.' Once you understand these laws and that All is Mind you become a *conscious co-creator*. If you want to know more about these laws check out this online course I have provided on the teaching platform Udemy: *www.udemy.com/ universal-laws (Apply this coupon code for a discount: theparadox)*.

In the book *The Light Shall Set You Free* authors Dr.

Milanovich and Dr. McCune talk about these laws referring to them as Divine Laws: *They are extensions of physical laws which apply to the spiritual world. They govern all planes of existence and the laws are interrelated.* [23] Understanding these laws will help us become conscious co-creators. Life on Earth is like a game where the masses have been playing without knowing the rules. Now the rules (The Laws) are being revealed and this allows for a whole new game to take place. Getting to know these Laws is a way to become God-realized. The time has come for these truths to become self-evident.

We have arrived at the part of the cycle of creation where some people re-member more about who we really are - about the set-up, the cycle and the universal laws and they are re-minding others. We are entering into the vibrational frequency of Aquarius and this has an effect on all of us. As Milanovich and McCune express:

The vibrational frequency of Aquarius (in the precession of the equinoxes) is of a higher note, vibrating closer to the speed of Light. As we enter this stage, the higher Light frequencies affect all on Earth. These vibrations are causing all systems that were built on lower frequencies (corruption, greed, lies, confusion, self-centeredness etc.) to fall........Thus we are witnessing "the end of the world" and we do not even recognize what we see. [23]

The Universal Laws - or ground rules - set up by The Mind will become more and more apparent to people all over the globe helping us to create consciously and from the heart instead of unconsciously and from the ego.

PEOPLE WITH POWER

Some people have known about these "playing rules" - these Universal Laws for a very long time and this knowledge has given them great power. They have played the game AND been aware of the "playing rules", but now these rules are being revealed to everyone. Part of the introduction to these laws on a mass scale came with the book and the movie *The Secret* in 2006. It focused on The Law of Attraction. This law is a secondary law resting on the Law of Vibration. The vibrations we send out are what is setting up the Law of Attraction.

Whatever you think and feel will cause vibrations and a specific frequency which is unique to you. This frequency is broadcasted out into the ether - into the sea of energy - and you get back what you send out. You are a vibrating sending tower broadcasting all the time. What you think and feel is setting up your personal vibration. If someone can control what you think and feel they can control your experience within this game. They influence your vibrational signals which in turn are being broadcasted out into the Universe giving you back what you sent out.

If you buy into fear it will influence how you think and feel. This in turn will set up your personal vibration which you broadcast into the ether. If you are worried and concerned you will attract more of this into your life because this is what you are sending out. The opposite is also true. If your thoughts and feelings are positive and happy you vibrate out a totally different vibration and good things will come into your life. Whatever you send out is based on what you think and feel. This is how God has set it up in order for God through you to experience what God wants to experience.

People have known about these Universal Laws and how they work for a long time. They have used this knowledge to gain power - power over the masses as long as we stay ignorant. They are ahead of many of the 'other players'in the game of life. As long as we *conform* they can control the masses and set up the vibrations which the masses will broadcast into the ether. As long as we buy into fear and keep reading and watching negative news we buy into their way of playing the game.

All Is Mind and 'these power people' are also part of The One Mind. So why are 'they' using different tools to keep 'us' at a low vibration? They are playing out their characters like actors in a movie. It´s all a game - a game of frequencies for The Mind to explore, to create, to do so it can *be*. As such God through 'they' wants to keep playing the game because it contributes to a range of experiences and emotions - from pain to pleasure. But we have reached a point where we don´t need to experience pain and suffering. We can move and hence these characters will no longer be needed. They have serves their purpose.

From the viewpoint of the soul going through pain and suffering in order to appreciate pleasure makes sense, but it´s very hard to accept as a human being. Many people suffer due to the way the   people with power play the game. Why endure suffering when we don´t have to? There is enough food and building material in the world to feed and shelter every single human being on Earth, but still some people are richer than certain countries. This makes no sense. Why are some people hurting and killing others to gain even more money and power? From the human being perspective this is insanity, but from the perspective of The Mind it´s part of the ongoing cycle - the movie with different characters.

Now we are on the threshold to a new world - a new era - a new 'compartment' within The Mind where there will be more unity. However, the individual aspect is still needed since The Mind needs interaction even at this 'new level.' Everything is Mind - consciousness - and it has to do something in order to be something. This evokes the souls, soul aspects. You can't do much by yourself. It's not much of an exploration of what consciousness may manifest as. It´s no fun playing a game all by yourself. You need interaction to experience several aspects of the game. This is mentioned by Gary R. Renard in his book *The Disappearance Of The Universe*: *In order for anything to interact you must have duality. Indeed, without duality there is nothing to interact with. There can be nothing in a mirror without an image that appears to be opposite it, attached to an observer to see it.* [5.1]

In order to interact the soul aspects have to think they are individuals. Some characters in this ongoing 3D game need to play the 'bad guys' and some characters need to play the 'good guys.' The dark and light. The world of duality and opposites. It´s part of the construct, but if you don´t realize it´s a set-up, a game, then your part will look like it´s real. You will think you are your body and that life is random - that it´s all about luck and coincidences. Most people are not aware of these Universal Laws which govern our lives and hence they easily use words like luck (good and bad) and coincidence to explain the ups and downs in life.

The French philosopher Voltaire (François-Marie Arouet) said that luck and coincidence are words that were invented to express the known effects of unknown causes. Some people seem to have the 'magic touch.' You've heard people say, 'Everything he touches turns to gold.' When we can´t find a reason for it, when we can´t find a plausible cause, when we can´t see how this is possible we turn to words like luck and coincidence. We are unable to see a logical connection and the only explanation we accept is that of luck and coincidence - like 'being in the right place at the right time.' Yet, it is the Law of Cause and Effect in action. Some people know about this law- others not. It´s one of the Laws in The Game of Life set up by The Mind - by God - by us since we all are God in Disguise. Remembering that we are not limited in our infinite state, but then we can't experience that state. You can then realize that this planet is actually the logical premise with intrinsic suffering that brings later appreciation and understanding. However the goal was not to suffer forever! We will be at some point exploring in a less limited way, experiencing some of the magic, this or it's not a true exploration of The Mind, is it?

THE GAME

What is currently going on in the world today is a game of frequencies. Some people with power know that all is energy and everything vibrates. They know about the Universal Laws that govern our lives. They know that thoughts and feelings are the navigational tools in this sea of energy. If they want to control people and keep them at a low vibration all they have to do is to influence them with different frequencies. This is the game. They control the masses through the use of different frequencies from media (TV, radio, internet), from pharmaceuticals, from food and drinks, through our water supply with fluorine, HAARP and much more. They have discovered what Nikola Tesla discovered:

If you want to find the secrets of the Universe, think in terms of energy, frequency and vibration.
- Nikola Tesla

We are now ready to wake up and realize we are God in Disguise and that All is Mind. Within this mind game you play a character, and waking up and realize this will change your life. It will change the game as it is supposed to do. However, since we are God in Disguise we know this on a deep level, but it has been hidden from us. We are not consciously aware of the set-up and our part in it. Now is the time to wake up and this is also why you are reading this book. If your character wasn't supposed to wake up you wouldn't be reading it. Something in you led you to this book and you decided to read it. What is this 'something?' It's God hiding in you.

More and more people will wake up now as the cycle inevitably turns and as such more and more people with power will lose their power as they are of the premise, not the future. They are the neo dinosaurs. The game - the movie - is changing. Part of The Mind - points of consciousness - are waking up - as they are supposed to. Certain characters realize that we are God in Disguise and they are re-minding others about who we really are. A planned awakening is going on. More people are "re-membering" since The Mind is solving the puzzle piece by piece as it was destined to do. It is the cycle of life. It is the rhythm, night - day, sleep - wake. However there are forces in place that wants to stop it. This is the resistance that causes time.

If we figured it all out too quick, if there was no resistance, then everything would be over before it began. Like when your chain comes off of your bicycle! The pedals spin free. The 'selfish people' are the con-seal-ment. The darkness (ignorance) that we are en-lightening via no-ledge. They want to continue to play this 3D game since they have 'the upper hand.' They have the power and control of the masses, but this power is slipping because of the awakening.

How do we as soul aspects wake up? By raising our frequency above the low frequency of fear. And what alleviates fear? Knowledge! When we do en-lighten we are no longer subject to the lower frequencies in the game. As Penny Peirce says in her book *Frequency - the Power of Personal Vibration*:

If your frequency is high, fast and clear life unfolds effortlessly and in alignment with your destiny, while a lower, slower, more distorted frequency begets a life of snags and disappointments. [22]

The Earth is now receiving energies of a higher nature via

understanding, something within is causing people to wake up to the fact that we are more than our bodies, the cycle turning. We are body, mind and soul. We receive spiritual energies causing our 'junk DNA' to be activated ('junk DNA' is noncoding DNA assumed to have no known biological function). We start to re-member who we are. These energetic frequencies coming into our atmosphere will as such affect our body, emotions and mind. We are at the end of a cosmic cycle and more energies are coming into Earth causing an upgrade in our vibrations. This cycle is part of the game we play. It helps people wake up - it´s helping The Mind wake up.

These cosmic cycles are also part of the space-time construct and now The Mind that fell will rise. We forget to re-member. These cycles are part of the plan to wake us up. It seems like we are given a window of opportunity to go on to the next level in this game. Just like a computer game with many levels. If you are stuck on one level you can´t move onto the next one. The only way to wake up and move on is to raise your vibrations, raise your game. This is why many spiritual teachers and channelers are talking about the different dimensions of creation being part of a scale of octaves. We must step it up in our vibrations to 'get over to the next dimension of creation.'

As more people wake up, the old energy and the people with power are becoming desperate to keep us at low vibrations. They need to keep us at a low, slow vibration to keep us in control. If we all wake up no-one will buy into the fear anymore and their methods of keeping us down will not be able to reach us. Someone with a high vibration cannot be affected by a low vibration. Low frequencies cannot exist in a field of high-frequency energy and awareness.

In the channeled book *The Light Shall Set You Free* authors

Dr. Norma Milanovich and Dr. Shirley McCune talk about frequencies and also about the Battle of Armageddon. They talk about forces wanting us to stay in lower frequencies and how fearful thinking filled with worry will rob our precious time in the present moment to create our future. These fearful thoughts rob us of our dreams and weaken us, for all thoughts based on fear slowly drain our Light. We are energy beings, and our mind controls the way in which we use this precious substance. They continue by saying:

In the Battle of Armageddon, opposing forces know this and work by whispering suggestions into your consciousness to encourage your mind to stay in lower states. When these forces see that your light is getting strong and you are no longer fooled, they move to a secondary plan. At this point, they begin to work through individuals around you whom they consider to be weak, fractured souls. These may include family members, coworkers, friends, or even acquaintances.

The negative forces know that if they can get these people to buy into these illusions they will become depressed, and will say things to you that plant seeds of doubt. Working through others, they hope eventually to get to you. The opposing forces frequently come through people whom you least suspect. Since everyone experiences ups and downs in life, these forces will wait until an individual is in a lower state of mind and then use that person to get to you. The Battle of Armageddon is being played out on the Earth plane. Unawakened individuals are mere puppets in this battle......it is an unseen battle between the sons and daughters of darkness and the forces of Light that has been prophesized for centuries. This battle is being played out primarily on the unseen planes of existence......

It is important to remember that dark forces HAVE NO POWER OVER YOU UNLESS YOU GIVE THE POWER TO THEM. The Light is all the protection that we need, as we are totally protected in the Christ energy. We have forgotten this momentarily because of the programming that for centuries has weakened us and moved us into a state of fear...

The dark forces challenge us and actually can bring out the best within us if we overcome the lessons and pass the tests that they bring us. Let them challenge you, but always keep your moment of power each instant of every day by holding the Light within and focusing on the purest and most positive thoughts your mind can create.[23]

These negative forces want to keep the game going since they are in control. It´s like playing chess with black and white chess pieces and the black ones are way ahead. However, the white ones don´t want to play anymore. They want to leave this part of the game behind. Enough is enough. No more re-incarnation to Earth to experience duality. Another level within The Mind is waiting. More people are waking up and re-minding others, but still the masses are asleep letting the people with power play the game as they see fit. Since we move along the cycle of life this part of the game will also be history.

Although on this subject Steve writes: 'Don't get too freaked by the good and evil thing, indeed the suggestion and misunderstanding of evil feeds fear, as in that they are keeping us down on purpose, they are the evil enemy out to get you? The enemy? In one mind? They are simply contrary programs. Before I woke I was more or less one of them, well, not as bad as they are! But making money, 'self-betterment' made perfect sense. I saw life as linear; A to B and of course B had to be a better place than A in accordance with the material concept of appreciation, expanding. As opposed to appreciation in the sense of valuing what you have. Another word code! So they are driven to succeed which they see as expansion rather than meaning, quantity rather than quality. So they are materialistic and that materialism is what is creating poverty. It's not a conspiracy of the devil; it's just two opposing mind sets creating resistance.

As we are raising our vibrations we move along. We 'go to a new level of consciousness. We start to experience a new area of The Cosmic Mind. This is the shift so many spiritual teachers are talking about - moving into the next dimension of creation and becoming aware that we are multi-dimensional beings all part of The Mind - God.

The people with power can of course raise their vibrations too, but they want to keep playing the frequency game in the 3D world and they use all means possible to keep it going. They like having power and playing the 3D game. They are ego based and not heart based. They have gone to great lengths to keep the game going, after all, what are they without their game? It´s easy to take a look behind the curtain once you know it´s all a game - a scene on a theater stage - set up by God - by yourself because you are acting out a soul aspect of God in order to experience yourself.

Most people are blind to all the cover ups done by these power people - cover ups like Area 51 and the UFOs all the way back to 1947, The Philadelphia experiment, 9/11, HAARP and the cause of different earthquakes, fluorine in toothpastes and drinking water to calcify the pineal gland which is the gateway to the spiritual realm, celebrity deaths, different vaccine programs and much more. It´s all about trying to control the 3D game, but the time has come to leave this "chess game" behind and start creating and experiencing on another level. In order to move on to this next level you can do the following:

1. Guard the entrance to your mind. Be aware and conscious of what you let into your mind and stop reading and watching negative news. Be discerning don't believe anything you don't understand.

2. Think of all the great things in your life and all you have to

be thankful for. Keep an attitude of gratitude. This will set up a higher vibration and cause you to get more to be thankful for.

3. Start to meditate and become aware of the energies around you. *Intent* is very important. Before meditating, state the intent to be more sensitive to these energies.

4. Be thankful for what you want to happen in your life as if it has *already happened*. See it vividly in your mind´s eye as something already existing.

5. Start thinking with your heart in all situations by always saying: What would *love* do now?

This will most certainly raise your vibrations and you will be out of reach from the lower frequencies. All the fear based methods by the power people will not be able to reach you. You will be getting ready to move into the next level of creation. And as Steve says: 'this book can help you in this because, via the understanding of what creation is, you can clearly see what it is not! So no, this planet was not created in order to go shopping!»

Everything is Mind and we are all in this Mind experiencing different parts of the finite world. We are living out different potentials of the infinite. We are God hiding from Himself. The so-called 'bad' people with power are also The One Mind - they too are God hiding. They are part of the whole construct too, but then they are of the premise only. If they came to the next levels they would simply recreate this reality They incarnate and reincarnate only on this level. They play out their part so don´t hate them. Just send them good, positive vibration. The light will always transform the darkness. These 'bad characters' play their parts because they are needed. The so-called dark forces challenge

59

us and can bring out the best within us.

It is the intention of this book to help people wake up. I play out my character and this is what I am supposed to do. The essence of who I am is consciousness - a soul aspect - playing the character Camillo who was born to be a spiritual seeker, gather information and share it. This book is one of many tools being introduced in the game to help God in Disguise wake up because many souls aspects are sound asleep. It´s time to wake up - to re-member.

We are moving into a part of the cycle where we can re-member more - once again become a member of The Cosmic Mind and be aware of it. We are learning, growing and evolving which is the same as "re-membering" who we really are.

CHAPTER THREE

LEARN, GROW, EVOLVE = RE-MEMBER

When we are aware we consciously grow as soul aspects of The One. Growing in this sense is re-membering. By re-membering we are once again - *re* - becoming a conscious *member* of the Cosmic Mind - re-member. We are moving along a cycle (or actually a spiral). We are on the ride and the further along we go the more we remember. It seems like growing, developing, evolving, learning, but it´s really remembering. The more you are able to remember dictates how many levels you can climb, the more levels you can climb the more you remember! Many talk of Earth as a school where we learn lessons and evolve. Yes in a way it can be explained as learning and evolving, but in truth it´s really re-membering, All That Is - The One Mind - does not need to learn anything.

All learning was already in His Mind, accomplished and complete.
- From The Disappearance Of The Universe by Gary R. Renard [5.1]

The One Mind knows everything about consciousness manifesting because it is already potential consciousness, but it needs the experience of it. *Being by Doing.* And it needs to blow the linear bubbles, so it has to re-experience itself, it's not creation, it recreation! In truth we are One Mind and The Mind is all knowing, but in order to interact with itself the soul aspects have to be different and the difference then comes via subtraction. The One Mind is the best at everything. For instance, it is the best painter, but then God does not bestow such genius on everyone. Only some characters in the play will be great painters. If everyone painted like Picasso then Picasso would not be Picasso. It´s not much of a game if all characters are the same. We need to be different characters and interact in order for God to get as much out of this game as possible. It's not a competition as the current world view suggests. So you don't have to be a superstar, all you have to be is happy and happiness is wherever you find it.

We are not learning about life, creation and God. Rather The Mind is 'allowing' us to re-member by moving along the cycle. It feels like learning, indeed the world feels real, but it's not. Learning is re-membering. We are all soul aspects of The One and we all have our parts to play. We are here to express our uniqueness. The more we play our part and express our uniqueness with passion and heart, the more we will re-member. We are here to create in order to experience so we can BE. We create with our thoughts and feelings. Our Universe is thought based. All is Mind and thoughts can become things.

In 1909 Thomas Troward (1847-1916) published a book based on a series of lectures he held in London called *The Dore Lectures*. Mr. Troward was an author and a judge in British-administered India with a special interest in mental science. After his retirement from the judiciary in 1896, he set out to apply logic and a judicial weighing of evidence in the study of matters of cause and effect. His works influenced the New Thought Movement. Here is an excerpt from his book *The Dore Lectures* regarding creation:

My mind is a center of Divine operation. The Divine operation is always for expansion and fuller expression, and this means the production of something beyond what has gone before, something entirely new, not included in past experience, though proceeding out of it by an orderly sequence of growth. Therefore, since the Divine cannot change it's inherent nature, it must operate in the same manner in me; Consequently in my own special world, in which I am the center, it will move forward to produce new conditions, always in advance of any that have gone before. [24]

Troward explains how God wants to create through the uniqueness of you, but most people don´t see it. One of the biggest challenges we face on this Earth today is ignorance. Ignorance is not the lack of study, ignorance is the ignore-ance of God. We don´t see the God power within us - the expression of God through us. As such many people are ignorant and instead of seeking answers, looking inside and exploring the incredible powers they have within - they just conform. They act like everyone else and this too has been part of the game, but now we have moved further along the cycle and anyone who wants to break free from ignorance should look into Trowards paragraph.

It can set you free from possible limitations you hold in your mind. You have great power within you since God is creating through you as Troward explains. First of all he says: *My mind is A center.* He doesn´t say *the* center. He says *a* center. My mind is *a* center, your mind is *a* center; everybody's mind is *a* center. How can that be? Since we are dealing with Mind there are no boundaries. When dealing with boundaries like in a room we can figured out the exact center of that room. It´s a mathematical certainty. However, when we are dealing with Mind there is not just *one* center. There are infinite numbers of centers. We are all centers - our mind is. All of us are part of The Divine, The Supreme, The All, The Everything, The Universal Consciousness, The Universal Cosmic Mind which goes on forever. We are part of the Infinite.
Troward goes on to say: *The Divine is always for expansion and fuller expression.*

In other words, it is for *creation, production*, onward, upward and forward. Hence drawing on the past and creating and making things better, bigger, greater and more productive. Yes, the Supreme Power, the Universal Consciousness always wants to express itself more through us. Hence we should always seek to explore our true potential because we have infinite power and infinite potential just waiting to get out so the Supreme Power can express itself better and more through *you*. This is the cycle. This is the process of re-membering, but how far will we go? Will we go full cycle and remembering everything?

I want to share what Steve told me in this regard: 'In theory we all have the potential to go full cycle, reach the sweet spots past this tough premise. But then only if you allow God, surrender to the higher wisdom. As long as you are dictating what your happiness will be, and that involves greed, you can't leave this place as your happiness is reliant on the domination of others, you are a cancer cell. But then you are already what God made you, so I am only really speaking to those who can hear and move. The others will think I'm crazy anyhow. The ones who understand will be able to stand under, connect with this knowledge. And that understanding will inspire and lift them to where a place they can reach. I am trying to en-courage people, remind people! It is what it is!'

We are particles of the universal consciousness - souls aspects - The Divine - The One Universal Mind and hence we have access to All That Is. You can do the impossible if you believe in yourself. Remember, The Divine Operation is on your side - it is part of you. The goal was joy! The pain had to come along as a byproduct, no one likes pain, well…You are God in Disguise. The One Mind is the expert on everything and it wants to reveal it through each and everyone of us, because it is each and everyone of us. Even the ones who unfortunately can't (or won't) make the shift. We should thank them in a way. Not feel sorry for them since they are designed to be greedy and they do get their money and stuff so.....they get their version of heaven even if it is at the expense of others. But then the others get theirs later. If you are true to who you really are and express it you will honor your soul contract - the reason you came this time around.

Furthermore, what we have experienced in the past will be used as building blocks to *produce something entirely new - not included in past experience.* Our past has made us who we are today and drawing on past experience will yield something new, something better, something more to express. The Supreme Power will operate through us because of its inherent nature and it will give us opportunities - *new conditions - always in advance of any that have gone before.* This Operation of Divine Mind is within us - we are A center of it. It is operating within us because we are part of the universal consciousness. We are within a Cosmic Mind experiencing the physical 3D world as an illusion - living out the potential. It's all about *expansion and fuller expression.* In his book *The Only Thing That Matters (Conversations with Humanity)* Neale Donald Walsch is saying the same thing:

Divinity is Patience and Kindness, Goodness and Mercy, Acceptance and Forbearance. Wisdom and Clarity, Gentleness and Beauty, Selflessness and Nobility, Benevolence and Generosity. And yes, so much, much more. You can imagine all of these things, you can think about all of these things, you can hold all of these things as ideas conceptually, but until you EXPRESS all of these things IN you, THROUGH you, AS you, you have not experienced Divinity. And you will never have an opportunity to experience these things unless Life PROVIDES you with such an opportunity. [25]

The No Thing wants to be Some Thing and through the construct of space and time it can express and experience its vast, unlimited, un-manifested potential through you, me and everyone else of the billions of soul aspects existing within this space-time reality. This urge for production, expression, growth and experience is the reason for our existence.

Our true role is to create endlessly from the infinite storehouse of possibilities located at the virtual level.
- Deepak Chopra

People with near-death experiences confirm this. They say the reason we are here is to attain spiritual growth which is to re-member. Since we are God in Disguise we want to express, develop, grow and experience our potential. As souls aspects we take on a body of flesh in the finite realm out of a desire for this expression, growth and experience. We are part of The Divine Plan where the potential is being lived out. The more we live it out the more we re-member who we are. We start playing the game and once in the game we want to qualify for higher spirit realms. We go through tests of initiation set out as part of the destiny path we chose before we were born. We are designed, we have personality. It´s like the life experiences test us to see what we have mastered and what we have forgotten - what we can accomplish and how far we can go.

It´s all about experiencing the potential of The Mind. The more we re-member the more we see other realities of The Mind. We move along the cycle. We want to explore the vastness of feelings - the complete spectrum - all the ways that consciousness may manifest and interact with itself. The driving force is e-motional. As long as The Mind experience's the complete spectrum of emotions then it's job done. As such, we as points of consciousness do what we can to make that happen. We want to stretch, expand, experiment and live out and manifest what The Mind already knows in terms of its potential.

But a potential is just that - a potential. How does it feel to live it out in the physical? It needs a 'physical container'- hence the set-up of the Universe as a playground, a doing environment, the space-time construct. Since we are playing the game we are also subject to its rules - the Universal Laws governing our lives. Laws like The Law of Vibration, The Law of Attraction, The Law of Cause and Effect, The Law of Polarity to mention a few. These laws are as real as the Law of Gravity, but where do they come from? Einstein once said this about the laws:

Anyone who becomes seriously involved in the pursuit of science becomes convinced that there is a spirit manifest in the laws of the universe, a spirit vastly superior to that of man.
- Albert Einstein

In his book entitled, *The Symbiotic Universe: Life and Mind in the Cosmos*, astronomer George Greenstein entertains the idea that a Supreme Being might be responsible for the Laws:

As we survey all the evidence, the thought insistently arises that some supernatural agency must be involved. Is it possible that suddenly, without intending to, we have stumbled upon scientific proof of the existence of a Supreme Being? [26]

In *Conversation with God* Neal Donald Walsch is asking God if it is possible to do what we want without fear of some sort of punishment - and God answers by telling him about the laws that govern the Universe, Laws laid down by God:

Neal: But if there is no hell, does that mean I can do what I want, act as I wish, commit any act, without fear of retribution?

God: The direct answer to your question is, yes, you may do as you wish without fear of retribution. It may serve you, however, to be aware of consequences. Consequences are results. Natural outcomes. These are not at all the same as retributions, or punishments. Outcomes are simply that. They are what results from the natural application of natural laws. They are that which occurs, quite predictably, as a consequence of what has occurred. All physical life functions in accordance with natural laws. Once you remember these laws, and apply them, you have mastered life at the physical level. What seems like punishment to you—or what you would call evil, or bad luck—is nothing more than a natural law asserting itself.

Neal: Then if I were to know these laws, and obey them, I would never have a moment's trouble again. Is that what you're telling me?

God: You would never experience your Self as being in what you call "trouble." You would not understand any life situation to be a problem. You would not encounter any circumstance with trepidation. You would put an end to all worry, doubt, and fear. You would live as you fantasize Adam and Eve lived - not as disembodied spirits in the realm of the absolute, but as embodied spirits in the realm of the relative....<u>The Laws of the Universe are laws that I laid down</u>. They are perfect laws, creating perfect function of the physical. [4]

The One Mind has created the space-time construct to facilitate itself - to help consciousness to create, experience and *be* through each and every one of us. We don't have to aggressively go out there and do great things, have great experiences as if life is a challenge.

Expressing yourself may be as simple a creating a humble garden. It's not a question of what you think you ought to be doing, it's a question of what you really want deep down. There are many examples in life where

people have fought tooth and nail to achieve what they assumed would be success, only to realize that they were happier before, the proverbial chasing of the dragon. Which really punches home the true meaning of the words written above the Temple of the Oracle at Delphi; know they self!
- Steve Berg

In this space-time construct we are governed by the Universal Laws - like the Law of Cause and Effect - we reap what we saw, but since we don´t re-member who we are and what this set-up is all about life seems random. We see it as a string of coincidences and luck (good and bad) resulting in the ups and downs in life. As previously mentioned the French philosopher Voltaire (François-Marie Arouet) said that luck and coincidence are words that were invented to express the known effects of unknown causes.

Yes, because we have forgotten who we are and how the Universal Laws govern our lives, but now we are once again re-membering and the laws are being revealed. This time is a time of awakening. More people are waking up and they are re-minding others. The construct and the laws are becoming apparent. We are re-membering.

We are moving into a higher frequency of the Aquarius and becoming conscious co-creators, our characters will become more relevant as the truth aligns with us as the cycle turns to cosmic spring. We had to forget in order to re-member, so part of the game is to re-discover higher knowledge in physical ways, to awaken and realize that we are all God in Disguise. As such we are all *one*. Each soul aspect has its own path - its own destiny but the goal is the same - evolving (re-membering) into the higher spirit beings we once were, but with individuality. And by doing this we gain experience which is needed in defining who we really are. In other words The Mind is defining itself - the No Thing is experiencing being Some Thing - Every Thing.

Experiencing and re-membering is the name of the game. Not learning. There is nothing to know, to learn. Every "thing" is a game designed to bring love which unfortunately evokes fear in order to define the said love. God already knows it all. It´s the potential of God, of The One Mind, that wants to be lived out through the doing and experiencing of it in the space-time construct. Earth is the playground where we come to in order to *create* - not learn. We know it all, but we (God) are lacking the experience. The learning, in-venting, dis-covering, is the doing part - the experience. We are realizing what we know through doing.

In order to experience being Some Thing we must go through the different emotions from pain to pleasure. Pain is unfortunately necessary in order to know what pleasure and happiness is. On our path back to re-membering we therefore also face darkness - we see the duality in play. Dark and light - pain and pleasure. The opposites. When we become aware of these Universal Laws and how they govern our lives we also realize that we are all One Cosmic Mind. We start spreading love, we bring light in a world of darkness. We just appreciate being part of this reality and start to enjoy the *now* - we play, love, laugh, and live out our uniqueness - our part of the game. We are safe and secure because we *know* we are God in Disguise. We realize that we are a unique piece of the puzzle and by living this out we complete the experience in this part of the cycle (the 3D reality).

THE AKASHIC RECORDS

Many spiritual teachers say that all we experience - all we feel while being here - is being recorded in what they call The Akashic Records (akasha is a Sanskrit word meaning "sky", "space" or "ether"). According to Kryon, an energy entity channeled by Lee Carroll, The Akashic Records are: *The energies of Gaia.* In Caroll´s book *The Twelve Layers of DNA* Kryon says that The Akashic Records is a Earth based attribute. He calls it a Cave of Creation - it is a real 3D cave, but also one with quantum attributes.

It is crystalline in nature and it will never be found due to where it is , how deep it is and the fact that it is hidden. No Human can ever enter it for it does not support human life as you know it. It contains a record of each and every soul that has ever been on the planet or is schedule to be on the planet. This is the quantum portion....The Cave of Creation is a planetary record of all Humans and therefore, is The Akashic Records of all humanity. Each soul has a crystalline record and each life time is imbued into the soul´s crystal. .....Many lifetimes are then etched upon one crystalline structure, representing the one soul that has incarnated many times. [27]

Some spiritual teachings say that The Akashic Records is stored in our so-called junk DNA, but what is junk DNA? After 13 years of research (Human Genome Project 1990 – 1993) carried out by top researchers from nations like USA, France, UK, Russia, Japan, Germany and more they came to the conclusion that only app. 2-10% of our DNA has a biological function - the rest, 90-98%, was called junk DNA – left-overs from evolution. However, Dr. Eugene Stanley and his team in the US and Dr. Peter Garajev and his team in Russia have researched this 90-98% of junk DNA. Independently they came to the same findings. This 90-98% is a biological language reacting to frequencies. Dr. Peter Garajev has also done extensive research into what he calls Wave Genetics showing that our DNA can be influenced by frequencies exposed to the body. He also says that this junk

DNA can communicate outside space and time. His team found out that our DNA can cause disturbing patterns in the vacuum, thus producing magnetized wormholes. [28]

Is this DNA then communicating with The Akashic Records? Kryon says that the DNA, unlike the cave, is personal. It carries the full Akashic Records of the *one human being* it represents. This record within the DNA is contained in the quantum, random chemistry and is not a linear representation of past lives. Instead it is an 'instruction set to connect to the main library' which is in a quantum state in what you would perceive as another dimension. It is only 'pointers' to the library, Kryon says.

So, yes what Dr. Peter Garajev and his team have found can very well be DNA communicating with the Akashic Records. Maybe this is the way for The Mind to 'store' all the experiences achieved through each soul and why some say they have the gift to access these Records. If this is the case then the day we leave this physical world all we have felt and experienced will be kept and stored similar to that of a hard drive in a computer, and these feelings and experiences are the ones we take with us when we die. This can be the reason why people with near-death experiences report seeing and feeling *all their lives* in what they call a life review. They access these records when they die. Steve explains it more in terms of a PC, the operating system and the added software, a bit like 'The Sims.' Each character is a program in itself, this in order for it to operate with the package, but then separation is an illusion, in truth it's one over-story.

In order for anything to manifest it must first be a concept in mind. The Mind retains a copy of the story. Why? Well it's a design, in order to achieve a goal, and the mechanics of that goal never change! As in; The Mind *has* to manifest/re-cognize in order to be. It *has* to forget in order to re-member, think, move, and it *has* to know pain in order to know joy. Therefore it's really a chain of inevitable eventualities, so you don't need a copy per se. This is why Steve never bothered to write any of this down. There's no need to. It's logic. It's a constant. Example: 1+1 is always 2, no need to write it down. What is the answer to 93818 x 498787? I have no idea, but I can 'work it out.'

We do know that there is an answer. It's simple math, logic. It exists somewhere out there in the infinite for now, but then we may need a calculator in order to retrieve it into the manifest. So, there's no need to keep a copy of the whole event, anymore than you need to keep a copy of every answer to every math problem, it can all be "worked out", retrieved as it is indeed a mathematical equation describing interaction. Kind of like that this book can be seen on screen as binary 01001000011010010010000001101000100. This is the math behind the manifest.

EARTH AS A PLAYGROUND

The Mind has set up the Earth as a "playground" in the space-time construct in order to live out its potential. The famous psychic Edgar Cayce - The sleeping prophet - touched upon this in one of his readings:

All souls come to Earth to test their spiritual ideals to see if they are real. Only by becoming subject to the physical influences of the flesh and the laws of the Earth realm can a soul know for certain if they really possess that spiritual ideal. Through this process, the soul is tested and the result is self-realization. This is the purpose of the Earth realm.[29]
Edgar Cayce

The Earth is a place to live out the potential - to enjoy the manifestation process because we have time to enjoy the process from idea to realization. We are souls - spiritual beings - conscious, thinking beings created in *the image of God*. Why? So God can realize and experience Himself. God wants to experience the physical - to bring out the vastness of potential and test it out in the finite world - on a planet like Earth. It is a great set-up - a great construct, because we can create and enjoy whatever we are able to think about.

Thoughts become things. Thoughts are energy and this world we live in is thought based - saturated with consciousness urging to experiencing itself. Since we possess *individual* consciousness we also come up with different ideas and thoughts. God acts through us and "gives us" different parts to play. Indeed if you are all one, alone, then what kind part is that to play, how is that freedom? As well as realizing that the feeling of air on your skin is part of what makes us feel free! So we need the construct.

We all represent The Mind and we come here to express the potential of The Mind. We are points of consciousness. The purpose is to live out whatever thoughts and ideas we resonate with and are passionate about. Live your truth, because everyone will anyhow. Obviously both Steve and I resonate with the content of this text. Steve says that it is the absolute truth, this as in that it never changes. But then some don't live in alignment with that truth. They are contrary by design. You can't help but play the part that was made for your character. Which again points to the fact that this book is not for everyone. Some have to call it rubbish via who they are.

If the Mind was seen metaphorically as water we would be like droplets that would be frozen and defined as a certain form in the finite space-time construct just like a character in a movie. When in reality water is one mass, an infinite sea. When an idea all of a sudden pops into your mind where does it come from? The answer is that you are resonating with some part of the infinite potential of God. God wants to experience Himself - God wants to 'get out' and feel and see how it is to be in the finite realm. God is setting everything up for Himself to be realized through you, me and everyone of us.

When you are being passionate about something it is the uniqueness in you wanting to be expressed. It´s your mission to express it. It is your character wanting to play its role, express itself, realize itself, reveal itself, and be acknowledged (feedback). Everyone wants to be seen, acknowledged as a valid living being, which stems from the core. A fractal of the same way that the One Mind wants to express itself, although that takes many souls interacting, but then it is indeed the same thing. Expressing your character is your sole purpose - your *soul* purpose. When you create from the heart - from passion you are doing what you came here to do. Many people feel this yearning inside to wake up and express their unique gifts and offer them in service to the world. They sense there is more to life - they are yearning for more life - more joy, more fulfillment and more purpose. It doesn´t mean that their lives up until now have been without meaning, that was the prep, the essential cosmic winter. Nothing is a co-incidence. Everything you have experienced was for the purpose of re-membering who you really are. To create yourself anew, but since we are unconscious co-creators we don´t see that.

You have a mission to complete - a soul contract. Many people feel this now. We experience a global awakening where the spirit inside of us wants to surface. The Universe evolves and remembers by giving. All That Is evolves by giving from its core and expressing it outward in the process of creating. The No Thing becomes Some Thing - Every Thing. All That Is expresses itself through you. It gives through you. The time has come to wake up and realize that you truly are God in Disguise and you are here to complete your soul contract - to complete the mission. To give and share your uniqueness with the world.

Without sharing your conscious spirit in your special way, you do not evolve spiritually. [30]
- Simion, The 7th Dimensional Light Beings.

If we choose to truly be ourselves instead of trying to be someone else we would help others be themselves too. Darryl Anka channels the energy entity Bashar and Bashar expresses this in a very good way:

The more you are yourself the more you actually will be capable of helping everyone else choose to be themselves. They will see, by your example, what they can also be. Not that they must choose it, but at least you give them the choice by choosing love, joy and excitement for yourself. And they do work. There is nothing in creation that contradicts the choices you make, that you believe most strongly are the ones that are your preference. There is no interruptions in your life. Everything is there for your reasons to use as you wish. Use them in the way you prefer to use them so they can be seen, felt and experienced in an en-riching way. And you will see and feel and hear and taste and smell. Everything will take its cue from that state of being. Be that state of being because you CAN. You don't need another reason to do so. Just BE who you are because that is who you are. That is reason enough in the eyes of Creation. You don't have to justify your existence, because if you did not deserve to exist you wouldn't. But you do exist and in the eyes of Creation it must be necessary - it must be important that you are a part of ALL THAT IS. Without you, without each and everyone of us - without every being in creation - without us all - ALL THAT IS

would not be ALL THAT IS. Be your part of ALL THAT IS -
Bashar [31]

The confusion comes via this ignorant reboot, where everything, everyone, it constantly subtly telling you to be something else? 'They' worship idols, pop stars, models and actors. Anyone with looks or money really, as superficial as you like! It's subtly suggested that if you are not like that, then you are a loser. But then it's really not that hard, simply stop being what you think they want you to be, what's accepted, and be yourself. And don't worry; we are all a bit quirky. And we like that, deep down we do. We must play our part in creation. We are here for a reason - to express our uniqueness - to manifest the potential of the No Thing into Some Thing.

P.M.H. Atwater died 3 times in 3 months in 1977 and in her near-death encounters she realized that we all have a special role or mission in life. In her book *We Live Forever* she says we play a unique part in the Divine Plan and we can express this part when we merge into or are cooperative with our soul. The will of every soul is to 'out-picture' the Greater Will as it is the soul that is responsible for carrying out God´s Plan for creation. [5] When we merge with our soul we discover that we are God in Disguise and we are here to create and experience in order to manifest the un-manifested. We have a purpose in this life. In her book *Keys to Soul Evolution* Jill Mara also touches upon the topic of a soul mission - a soul contract. She says:

In this life, you are a composite of certain chosen aspects of your soul, expressed in a particular way this time around. In this life, you are seeking fulfillment in the areas that you have not yet experienced. You are branching out and expanding your soul. In order to raise your vibration, you need to stretch your frequency..........it is not the new car that raises your vibration in the long term. It may be what you had to do to get the car..............it is not the material things possessed that will give your soul satisfaction. It is the process of challenging yourself to transform that will truly give you the elation you seek. [30]

In other words God, through the soul aspects that we are, creates and experiences more of its potential. By doing this we evolve as souls - we re-member more of who we are. We create ourselves anew. When we continually grow and expand (re-member), we brighten our representation of All That Is. We are helping No Thing becoming Some Thing. The purpose is to create our experience—and thus, create ourselves anew. Another version of what we come here to do is also found in the work of my good friend and spiritual teacher and artist Bryan De Flores. Here is an excerpt from his spiritual work called *The Masterworks - Explorations in Spiritual Magic*:

Before you arrived on Earth in this lifetime, you, as a soul, with assistance from your Guardian Angel and the "Hall of Records" Council, created a chart and contract for this lifetime. This chart was configured very meticulously; taking into consideration everything that you wanted to learn and do, as well as planning the timed insertion of all of your skills and talents from previous incarnations.

In addition, any accumulated positive and/or negative karma was written into the chart as 'experiences' (relationships/friends/family, financial difficulties/prosperity, etc.) in order to either clear it or to enhance and "magnify" your life in some way. All family members and nearly all friends and brief acquaintances were very specifically chosen by you in order to maximize your experience here on Earth.

And although your chart unfolds in '"set-in-stone" fashion, it does accommodate lateral movement and spontaneity within each experience. For example, you will determine how easy or difficult and how long or short a given experience may be; depending upon the choices you make and how you handle all facets of each situation. Consequently, it is important to understand that all of this preplanning was designed to assist you to manifest your highest potential as the human and spiritual being here on Earth. [32]

In other words we have a destiny and a path to walk or a part to play as also P.M.H. Atwater touch upon in her book *We Live Forever:*

You are destined to do certain things in life, and within that destiny is choice as to how well, how consciously you will do something or you will be in that relationship or you will solve the challenges in your life or you will pursue your creativity. [5]

Our destiny is to do - to create - to let God´s potential out and hence we are all soul aspects - points of consciousness doing the will of God because in the end we are all God in Disguise. To be conscious of our destiny and manifest it we must go within. Why? Because within we find the inner voice and feeling always present and guiding us. How many times do you ignore your gut feeling and then stand and watch as everything goes wrong? 'I knew I should have listened to myself!' When we find stillness and stop the external world - stop its constant noise and buzz - we give room for the inner world to show us what to do - what to create. It brings us sight. In-sight. However in our busy world we let our five senses suck up everything that is being thrown our way from TV commercials, news about world catastrophes and crime to TV reality shows based on drama. We don´t let the inner world show us - no in-sight. We are too busy being occupied with the external world. We don´t see that *going within* is the key. Why? Because we had to forget in order to play the game. We all have individual consciousness and we have to forget in order to create ourselves anew.

It must seem like new perspectives this time around. If

we did remember everything this game would be pointless. Without forgetting the 'You Are God in Disguise' part we would not be able to play this game. However, now it is time to re-member. So many signs are being revealed to us from ancient scriptures, spiritual teachers and indigenous people all saying - *go within*. And more than that, we do actually retain a subconscious remembrance of who we are, we are born with personality.

It's just that we don't have a tangible framework in order to define/understand why we are the way we are. That's what life's for, so we can see why we choose what we do, this as we see and experience the ramifications of choices that don't suit us. When you go within you create from your heart which is what you are supposed to do. You can create whatever your heart desires for the benefit of yourself *and* others. In order to create we much first have an idea of what to create and these ideas come to us from The One Cosmic Mind. It is seeking an outlet for its potential - wanting to manifest it through us.

When you get an idea you are passionate about it is the soul aspect of you seeking creation and manifestation. You have the power to manifest the ideas that come to you since you are God in Disguise. You resonate with the ideas and you can bring them out into the space-time construct. You are also here to enjoy this manifestation process while it lasts - enjoy the experience from the first time the ideas pop into your mind until they are manifested. This is something Wallace D. Wattles wrote about back in 1910 in his book entitled, *The Science of Getting Rich*. He says:

God, the One Substance, is trying to live and do and enjoy things through humanity. The Source says: I want hands to build wonderful structures, to play divine harmonies, to paint glorious pictures; I want feet to run my errands, eyes to see my beauties, tongues to tell mighty truths and to sing marvelous songs. All that there is of possibility is seeking expression through men. God wants those who can play music to have pianos and every other instrument, and to have the means to cultivate their talents to the fullest extent; He wants those who can appreciate beauty to be able to surround themselves with beautiful things; He wants those who can discern truth to have every opportunity to travel and observe; He want those who can appreciate good food to be luxuriously fed. He wants all these things because it is Himself that enjoys and appreciates them; it is God who wants to play, and sing, and enjoy beauty, and proclaim truth and wear fine clothes, and eat good foods. It is God that worketh in you to will and to do. The desire you feel for riches is the infinite, seeking to express Himself in you. [3]

This is it. No Thing wants to be Some Thing. The Mind wants to stretch its legs, go for a walk, but it has no legs and nowhere to walk. It wants to move around, do something, be something so it creates this illusion - this hologram - the space-time construct in order to do just that. All is Mind - it´s all a construct - not real, but it sure does feel real when you are a human being. But then the body is just the vehicle used by consciousness to gain the experience. Everything we see is an illusion - we live inside a hologram as scientists are finding out. They are trying to catch up and figure out creation and our reality, but they will never see the full picture as long as they use logic and only logic. In their defense, science has done more for this awakening that religion ever has! Religion just sits on it's hands in the face of the evidence that sciences digs up. Science puts the work in, enquires, but then yes, logic in itself is not enough.

God is bigger than science and logic because God is also magic. When trying to see God we have to realize that we see it in terms of a linear understanding, which means we are already too late. God is all and instantaneous, so if you are adding things up you are way too slow, you are fragmented. Everything happens now - in The Mind. And The Mind is the hologram we live in - The All - and it is also the potential not yet manifested - the No Thing. God - The Mind - is All and Nothing.

People with near-death experiences often report being one with everything. They talk about being everything, everywhere, every time. Infinite and undying - no distinction between 'I'and everything else - The Universe. They are One with All That Is. Is this proof that All is Mind? Can we rely on near-death accounts to verify that everything we think is real is actually an illusion - that we are in fact God in Disguise living out the unlimited, un-manifested potential of God?

CHAPTER FOUR

NEAR-DEATH EXPERIENCES

P.M.H. Atwater is one of the most well-known researchers in the field of near-death experiences (NDE). In 1977 she died three times in three months - January 2nd, January 4th and March 29th. These three NDEs made a big impact on her. Eventually it led her to finding people with similar experiences. She began her NDE research and has in total interviewed more than 3,000 people with NDEs. In her book *We Live Forever* she talks about how the meeting with The Light, with God, completely changes you as a person and what you perceive as reality:

The Light is the very essence, the heart and soul, the all-consuming consummation of ecstatic ecstasy. It is a million suns of compressed love dissolving everything unto itself, annihilating thought and cell vaporizing humanness and history, into the one great brilliance of all that is and all that ever was and all that ever will be. You know it´s God. No one has to tell you. You know. You can no longer believe in God, for belief implies doubt. There is no more doubt. None.

She goes on to say:

You know you are a child of God - a cell in the greater body, an extension of the One Force, an expression from the One Mind. No more can you forget your identity or deny or ignore or pretend it away. There is One and you are the One. [5]

This is what The Light does to you, she says. You are reborn because at last you re-member. As she says: *You are an expression from The One Mind.* Yes, this is what is going on here on Earth. We express the potential of The One Mind. We manifest the un-manifested and make it 'real' in the time-space construct. There is only one of us here. One Mind - All and No Thing. The majority of the people she interviewed in her NDE research said they became one with everything - they had no physical body awareness - they simple existed, but with what many refer to as a light body or a spiritual body. They never died - only transformed. Atwater also refers to the Aramaic word for death which translates - *not here, present elsewhere.*

When we die we leave the body behind, but it doesn't mean we are gone forever. Being out of sight is not the same as being out of mind. All is Mind and The Mind never dies - it just experiences different 'parts' of itself. When we die we simply 'shift' to another experience within The Mind. We are still conscious and aware after we die. We are conscious beings and when the body dies the consciousness continues. Gary R. Renard also mentions this in his book *The Disappearance Of The Universe.* He says:

What you call this side and the other side are really just two sides of the same illusory coin. It's all the universe of perception. When your body appears to stop and die, your mind keeps right on going. [5.1]

The body is the vehicle or the container used by consciousness to experience itself. If you drive a car and the car breaks down you leave the car behind and continue your journey. The same with consciousness. The body breaks down and dies, but the driver, consciousness, moves on. Just like in the movie Avatar. The main character, Jack Sully, moves his consciousness from his Earthly body to the body of The Avatar. It is still the consciousness of Jack, but he is experiencing himself through another body.

We are all part of a Cosmic Mind - what many call God. This Mind is conscious. We are as such points of consciousness having a physical experience. You are a point, I am a point - everyone is a point of consciousness and we are all connected since we are The One Mind. This can be illustrated using the analogy of a digital picture.

A digital picture consists of tiny pieces of information called pixels - picture element. A pixel is the smallest controllable element of a picture. It is a little dot - like a point - of the picture and together with all the other points (dots) they are making up the image. You, me and everyone else are just like pixels. We are points of consciousness and together we represent The One Mind. We, as pixels, represent The Grand Picture of The Universe. Indeed everything is relative, how can you be a husband if you don't have a wife?

Nothing makes sense unless supported by its relative definers, and note here that it takes a whole universe in order to define the concept of a human being. When we don't know who we are we don't see the connection and we go about our life thinking we are separate from everyone else. We think we are just this tiny pixel disconnected from all the other pixels - from the rest of the world.

However, when you raise your vibrations you expand your consciousness. It is similar to zooming out from the one pixel point that you are. You start to see a pattern. You begin to understand you are part of something bigger and the more you expand your consciousness the more you "zoom" out and see the 'bigger picture.' You see how you and the other pixels together make up the One Grand Picture of All That Is. This is what is going on now. We are waking up realizing that we are indeed important points of consciousness representing The One Mind. We are all connected. In fact, everything is connected even the galaxies in our Universe as explained in a channeled message from Kryon through Lee Carroll:

Every galaxy has a push/pull system at its center. This is a twin energy system, but you only are aware of one. You're convinced it's invisible, and it's a black hole. No light escapes, but you think it's singular - one thing...It is not one thing. Instead, it's a beautiful, double eye of a needle...

...Picture with me for a moment a giant needle and thread, two of them. One goes into the black hole and one comes out of it. These threads are inter-dimensional strings of force that connect themselves to the other galaxies, weaving in and out of their centers, which are all double-eyed black holes. A push and a pull - an inter-dimensional force of which you are not aware of yet, threading the galaxies one to another and to another. [59]

Everything is connected because all is Mind, but while we are here on Earth we don´t remember being part of this Mind - this consciousness. We perceive ourselves to be separate from everything else. Deep down we know we are all connected since we are all part of this One Mind. Our intuition is the key. It knows. Our intuition is our connection to this Mind.

People with NDE say they are one with everything. Yes, because on Earth they are experiencing this one point of consciousness, but when they die, they once again re-member and see how they are connected to the entire consciousness field - The whole Mind. It is like they only see themselves as a single pixel of the One Grand Picture of All That Is when they are in their human bodies on Earth, but when they die they become aware that they are in truth the whole picture. They are connected to ALL the pixels - to the whole Mind. In truth we never "leave" The Mind - we just forget who we really are and our connection to it.

Steve explains how The Mind creates the appearance of matter and separation like this: "The appearance of matter is achieved via micro points of energy changing polarity, as all energy is forced to due to the paradox. So it's an oscillation, not a vibration as science has suggested. Vibration is movement, and that requires mass, but the Mind has no mass! Indeed it is oscillating from positive to negative in order to create a 'differential' con-trast, to then create the borders that define mass - matter.

Therefore at base everything is one blanket energy field. Which means that your brain is your car, is your cat, is your guitar. It's only the varying frequencies at which the energy is oscillating that creates the appearance of matter, and science used to champion that theory, before the money grabbing search for the boson, jobs for the boys! If the Universe seems to contain consciousness, with separation being an illusion, then ergo, the Universe must itself be conscious!

The interference comes via the vague suggestion that the boson is the building block of the Universe. The finite particle? What, a solid ball of matter? It makes no sense! Think of it this way, if you could magnify the boson to the relative size of a planet. And then stand on it, 'they' are saying that there's 'nothing' below the surface you are standing on? This is the small end of space? Well that's a whole lot of nothing. Infinity runs both ways, macro and micro and no one in their right mind would look for the large end of space. The large end would be a massive wall? So what's on the other side is the question that immediately springs to mind as there is so much of it?

The reason they look for the small end is really lame. It's because it can't be seen, a simple case of out of sight out of mind. 'Under rug swept»! With the truth being that the finite particle and the large wall at the end of space would be in fact the exact same thing, boundaries. Begging the question what's beyond, what's a boson made of? If they could see a boson, all they would see is an energy sphere appearing and disappearing, an oscillating pixel for all intents and purposes.

But then they have trouble getting a good look at a quark! They don't have the technology to see any further, the particles are too small and too fast. And as for the large end of space? Well that's like trying to find the end of your own mind. You see space and man are one mind, the man is a sole aspect and the universe is the stage, the reflected reality, but it's all one mind. Like that if you imagine a landscape with people in it, that picture is just one mind - imagination. The concept of a man doesn't make sense without the supporting 'reality.' So everywhere a man goes there will be space."

Another well-known researcher in the field of NDE is Dr. Raymond Moody. He is a psychologist and medical doctor. He has written many books about life after death and near-death experiences (NDE), a term he coined in 1975 - the year he released his book *Life After Life*. It became a best-seller with millions of copies sold worldwide. The book focused public attention on the near-death experience like never before. Raymond Moody has spent nearly 40 years looking forward, trying to understand what happens when people die and has talked with over a thousand people who have had these NDE. Since the 70ties we have seen a huge increase in reports on NDE. Millions of people from all walks of life and from all corners of the world report having been on 'the other side.' They talk about how they left their body behind to experience another realm of existence.

Thanks to people like Atwater, Moody and other great spokespersons in the field of NDE more and more stories about people with these experiences have seen the light of day. Some of the other researchers and spokespersons I would like to mention are Bruce Greyson, Kenneth Ring and Peter Fenwick. Bruce Greyson is a Professor of Psychiatry at the University of Virginia. He is the co-editor of *The Handbook of Near-Death Experiences* that was published in 2009. Kenneth Ring is Professor Emeritus of psychology at the University of Connecticut, and a researcher within the field of near-death studies.

Ring is the co-founder and past president of the International Association for Near-Death Studies (IANDS -

1981) and is also the author of several books on NDE. One of them is *Mindsight: Near-Death and Out-of-Body Experiences in the Blind* where the book investigates the astonishing claim that blind persons, including those blind from birth, can actually 'see'during near-death or out-of-body episodes. Dr Peter Fenwick is a neuropsychiatrist and neurophysiologist who is known for his studies of epilepsy and end-of-life phenomena. He is recognized as an authority on the relationship between the mind and the brain. He is also the author of several books one of them being *The Truth in the Light - an investigation of over 300 Near-Death Experiences*.

Thanks to these people and others like them more and more attention and focus is being given to the field of NDE. Why? Why is this happening now? Are NDE a recent phenomenon? No, it´s not a new phenomenon. A great number of them have been recorded over a period of thousands of years. We find stories with NDE resemblance in ancient text and religious books. We also find evidence of this in the work of the Greek philosopher and mathematician Plato (427-347 BCE). But why are we seeing a growing interest in this field now - in our life time? Why do we find an emerging interest for spiritual information in books and films about the afterlife? Because it´s time.

We are ready to take in a new truth as also Steve has explained to me. There was no way that this concept could have been understood until now, why, because we didn't have the language in order to describe it. Noting that our true language is our reflected reality, the words we use are just labels for things and descriptions of interactions. You can easily see that we were waiting for technological advance, which can then be used in order to provide example in order to explain such complex concept, our truth. PC technology, medical understanding that explains how our experience of reality is not direct, it's fly by wire! Movies such as The Matrix which bring such concepts to life, this is all play and learn! Yes, we can now describe the cycle, well someone also had to experience it, but we do now have the language.

We are waking up and people with NDE are important characters in this movie of life - in the book - in the story that is being lived out in a linear fashion with past, present and future. They are coming forth with their stories since this is part of the plan to wake up and see that we all come from The Cosmic Mind and that other realities beyond our 3D world also exist. People with NDE are re-minding others that we are all connected and that love is the glue that holds everything together. As the story keeps playing out - as the cycle moves on - even new characters and new phenomena are being revealed. One of them is the phenomenon called *shared NDE*. This is a phenomenon where a NDE is actually shared by someone who is not dying, but who is emotionally connected or in close proximity to someone who is concurrently in the 'life/death' transition.

Dr. Raymond Moody began to hear about these shared-death experiences in the 1980´s when he was doing his NDE research. Friends, family, and medical personnel go along with the dying as they are surrounded by the light, taken through the tunnel, and sometimes even take part in the life review. Together with author Paul Perry Dr. Moody wrote the book *Glimpses of Eternity (published October 2010)* which was the first book to talk about the phenomenon of shared death experiences, this common, but mysterious experience of family and friends sharing a loved one's journey from this life to the next. This type of experience is becoming increasingly reported. Why? Because it is yet another piece of the puzzle helping us re-member who we really are. We are waking up. We are moving along the cycle of remembrance and more and more people will wake up and see that we are all part of this

One Cosmic Mind - The Mind of God. We are points of consciousness using the physical body as a container to create, do and experience in order to be. We never die we only transform and experience other 'realities' of The One Mind.

In 2011 several people with NDE were featured in a documentary called *AfterLife*. It was released by bestselling author Paul Perry. Back in 2005 he started his own production company with the goal of making innovative documentary films that matter and *Afterlife* is one of them. It is a study about the great question: *what happens when we die?* Answers to this question are examined in a study of the near-death experience (NDE) and the inescapable conclusion is reached, that there is no need to fear death: There is an afterlife. One of the people being interviewed is Jenny Somers and her NDE has convinced her that we are all part of a Cosmic Mind. She says:

We reconnect to a Universal Mind. Here (on Earth) we are like "unplugged from our Source" and we take our plug and try to plug it into each other and to things hoping that the person is going to make me happy or that the car is going to make me happy. We keep trying to draw energy from people and things in this dimension, and every time we take that plug and we connect it back to our Source, then we become full and then we become connected. [57]

In the documentary Raymond Moody is also interviewed and when being asked the question: *what happens when we die?*, he answers:

We enter into another state of existence - or another state of consciousness that is so extraordinarily different from the spatial and temporal frame of reality in which we exist in the physical world that the language we have is not yet adequate to describe this other state of existence or consciousness. [57]

Yes, it is another state of existence where people with NDE have gone through a so-called life review. They see and feel all their lives and how their actions touched other people both good and bad. There is no judgment. No karma in the sense that you are being punished and have to experience the "bad stuff" you did to others. Karma is not a punishment, rather it is a remembering experience designed to help us move on to higher levels of spirituality. Only by re-membering that we are all connected, like cells in a body, will we stop hurting each other. I want to share what Steve told me regarding this topic:

The 'judgment' when you die is simple. You see or sense oneness and in that you see that you have been fighting yourself. Why would you do that? The oneness creates a deep empathy, you feel connected, and so you feel all the pain of each action.

There's only one of us here and when we die we will sense the oneness. People with NDE change how they think and feel when they 'come back to Earth' after sensing this oneness. Many of them say that the most important thing we can do while we are alive is to learn how to love. Love holds everything together and many NDE accounts talk about how they felt encased in love when they left their bodies and experienced 'the other side.' It was an all-inclusive love. No judgment whatsoever. Why? Because the life we play out on Earth is an illusion designed to live out and experience the unlimited Love of God. Of course it's unlimited love, why? Because it's actually self-love!

We are all playing a character in this movie called life and when we die we leave our mask (ego) behind and the essence of who we are moves on. We play characters just like an actor in a movie, but when the movie is over the actor goes home just like we go home when the "acting on planet Earth" is over. Home being "The Cosmic Mind with all its "compartments". Jesus said: *in my Father's home there are many*

mansions if it were not so I would have told you so. People with
NDE seem to tap into these different 'mansions' or levels.
They are having an experience in one small part of "this huge
house of the Father" - The One Cosmic Mind. When we once
again connect with this Mind we sense oneness and pure love.
We are not being judged for the actions of the characters we
play out. They are important characters - both 'good and bad.'
Without the 'bad' we wouldn´t know what 'good' is.

People with NDE know they are an expression of The
One Mind, but what about the rest of us without any NDE to
account for? Most of us have forgotten who we really are and
we have no experience of this oneness re-minding us. As a
previous atheist I could never accept life after death. I thought
life was random and when the body died it was over. After
years of research in the spiritual field I totally agree with
authors like Atwater, Moody, Perry and people with near-
death experiences saying that All Is Mind and that we are part
of this Mind. We are God in Disguise and we never die, we
only transform. For some this information will resonate, but
for others it will not since it can´t be proven.

There is no point in trying to convince a skeptic and an
atheist about life after death. No proof in the world will be
good enough. They have to experience it for themselves or
decide to do what I did - spend years of research looking into
what the spirit world really is. I opened my eyes and found a
bridge between science and spirituality. I never had any near-
death experience to re-mind me of who I really am. After
days, weeks, months and years of research I arrived at the
same conclusion as those with a near-death experience. There
is an after-life. We continue our journey. We are still conscious
after we die and very much aware of the other realties we
encounter beyond this one.

More people are waking up and changing their take on life
and the afterlife. More and more research is getting out into
the public arena showing people that we live in a thought

based Universe and that death is just a transformation. One person who completely shifted his view of the afterlife is Dr. Eben Alexander. In October 2012 he published his book *Proof of Heaven*. He is a neurosurgeon who found himself in a coma, he experienced things he never thought possible— a journey to the Afterlife. He says:

As a neurosurgeon, I did not believe in the phenomenon of near-death experiences. I grew up in a scientific world, the son of a neurosurgeon. I followed my father's path and became an academic neurosurgeon, teaching at Harvard Medical School and other universities. I understand what happens to the brain when people are near death, and I had always believed there were good scientific explanations for the heavenly out-of-body journeys described by those who narrowly escaped death. There is no scientific explanation for the fact that while my body lay in coma, my mind—my conscious, inner self—was alive and well. While the neurons of my cortex were stunned to complete inactivity by the bacteria that had attacked them, my brain-free consciousness journeyed to another, larger dimension of the universe: a dimension I'd never dreamed existed and which the old, pre-coma me would have been more than happy to explain was a simple impossibility. [33]

Eben Alexander said he had no body awareness - no arms or legs. He experienced 'another part' of The Cosmic Mind - something totally unthinkable when he was the old - pre-coma Eben. This is a clear example of a black dot turning into a red dot. His truth changed. He now sees reality from a totally different perspective.

This experience changed him. Mr. Alexander has already faced skeptics challenging his story about this other realm of existence and if his experience was real. These skeptics are the black dots trying to pull him into the black frame of 'truth' because they 'know' heaven doesn't exist. They say his brain was not completely shut down and it 'played tricks' on him. These skeptics use logic and science and don't realize that this is not enough to comprehend the mystery of creation. Logic and science are the tools we use to understand the finite realm. It can never be used to understand the whole of creation. All is Mind and people with experiences from "the other side", like Dr. Alexander, are helping us understand this. They are essential characters helping us re-member who we really are - God in Disguise. We are magical at base since creation is a paradox - the infinite and the finite - magic and logic hand in hand (more about that in chapter nine The Paradox of Creation).

My good friend Barbara With is an author, composer, performer and psychic. Her book *Imagining Einstein* is a channeled book where she claims to have channeled Einstein. Einstein speaks through her. The following is an excerpt from her book on the topic of the AfterLife:

What is the urge to create human life that then becomes you, him or her? To begin with, accept that the answer to this question is rooted in mystery. Even from AfterLife, the point or origin is obscured. What or who stirs where all possibilities exist simultaneously in the nothingness to manifest into matter in a particular way is an enigma. [34]

Yes, creation is a mystery - an enigma - because it´s more than logic. It´s also magic and one cannot use logic to explain the magic of creation. Barbara also says: *Nothingness manifest into matter.* Yes, this has been the main theme of this book - the No Thing has an urge to be Some Thing - to experience - express - feel in the physical plane. It does this through the soul aspects who use the human body as a vehicle on planet Earth. But how has The Mind set up the construct in order for the soul to navigate the human body? Through electromagnetic tools called thoughts and feelings which again is subject to the Universal Laws governing the whole universe.

Whatever we set up as a vibration is a signal to The Mind saying what we want to express and experience. The Laws make sure we get what we need in order to gain whatever experience we want. People, situations, events come into our lives and they seem to appear by chance - by coincidence. There are no coincidences in The Mind - it's all part of the construct. We attract into our lives what we think about and what we give energy to. However, research is showing that we are controlled by our subconscious mind in how we think, feel, react and behave. As such it may seem like life is more or less random, but it's not. It is a very clever set-up by God to make this game work.

CHAPTER FIVE

THE POWER OF THE SUBCONSCIOUS MIND

Have you every decided to think more positive thoughts in order to change your life in a more positive direction? Did it work? For most people it doesn´t. They don´t get the results they want. The creation process is often a struggle. We typically meet a lot of resistance in making our dreams come true. In 2006 the book The Secret was published and it quickly became a bestseller all over the world. It focused on one of the Universal Laws existing in this Universe: The Law of Attraction. With positive thinking we can attract into our lives what we want. Many people tried this, but failed to get the results they wanted. Why? Didn´t the message in the book get across to the reader? That´s not it. The reason many fail in attracting what they want into their lives and making their dreams come true has to do with vibrations and the subconscious mind. The Law of Attraction rests on the Law of Vibration. Whatever we vibrate out is what we attract to us. The vibration you are emitting right now is set-up by your subconscious mind and for most people it goes unnoticed. We are not aware of it. The subconscious mind is "running the show". It´s in the 'driver´s seat'of your life.

The cover of the US News and World Report on February 28, 2005 was entitled: *The Secret Mind: How your Unconscious Really Shapes your Decisions.* It stated:

We are conscious of only 5% of our cognitive activity, so most of our decisions, actions and behavior depend on the 95% of the brain activity that goes beyond our conscious awareness. [35]

This report clearly illustrated how the subconscious mind controls our decision making process and ultimately our lives. Current research suggests that we are only conscious of even less than 5% of our cognitive activity. It suggests that we are only conscious of 3%. As such 97% goes beyond our conscious awareness.[36] Is it then a coincidence that app. the same percentage - 96% - of the Universe is dark - dark matter (73%) and dark energy (23%)? The Law of Correspondence embodies the truth that there is always a correspondence between the laws and phenomena of the various planes of being and life - 'As above, so below; as below, so above.' So what we find in the micro cosmos will be present in the macro cosmos. As human beings we are at the mercy of our subconscious mind and on a bigger plane it seems that The Cosmic Mind is too. In other words it is not aware of what is going on because *we* are not aware of what is going on. When we start to wake up then the Cosmic Mind will wake up. We are moving along a cycle from forgetting to re-membering.

Since we are at the mercy of our subconscious mind the question we have to ask ourselves is this: Is our subconscious mind thinking positive or negative thoughts? How is it programmed? This will determine what we vibrate out into the Universe - to The Mind and ultimately what we attract into our lives. The programming starts when we grow up as Prof. Bruce Lipton talks about in his book *Spontaneous Evolution*:

Our fate is under the control of recorded programs or habits that have been derived from instincts and the perceptions acquired in our life experiences. The most powerful and influential programs in the subconscious mind are the ones that were recorded first. During the extremely important formative period between gestation and six years of age, our fundamental life-shaping programs were acquired by observing and listening to our primary teachers - our parents, siblings, and local community. Unfortunately, as psychiatrists, psychologists, and counselors are keenly aware, much of what we learned was based on misperceptions that are now expressed as limiting and self-sabotaging beliefs. [37]

Research shows that from the time we are born until we are six years old our brain waves are in the two lowest brainwave states theta and delta. At these levels there is *no conscious filter.* Being in these levels allow us to download massive amounts of information. As adults we go through all the different brain wave states every night. When we are awake we are in Beta brain wave state - focused consciousness. When we slow down our brain waves by meditating or when going to sleep we move into the Alpha brain wave state - 8-12 Hz. At this state we have calm consciousness.

Jose Silva researched these states for 40 years. He discovered that we have the ability to influence our subconscious mind while being in the alpha state. When we move further down in brainwave activity we reach the Theta level where the frequency range is from 4-8 Hz.

At this level we are below consciousness. This is also true for the lowest level - the Delta state with a frequency range from 0.5-4 Hz. This means that from birth until six years old we operate at brain wave activity levels below consciousness - no conscious filter. As such the 'truths and values' being 'fed' to us during these first six years has a powerful effect on us.

Delta and Theta brain frequencies define a brain state known as hypnotic trance - the same neural state that hypnotherapists use to directly download new behaviors into the subconscious minds of their clients. In other words, the first six years of a child's life are spent in a hypnotic trance. [37]
- Bruce Lipton

Why would The Mind - God - create us in this way? Why is

there no conscious filter from birth until we are six years old? What is the point? There must be a reason for this set-up. Some spiritual teachers talk about how the human life divides into seven year segments or cycles, during which certain physiological and psychological changes take place. They also say that during the first seven years we grow up we get our major imprinting. This is very much in line with what Bruce Lipton is talking about. We are being programmed. We are being shaped and molded. It's an imprint. This imprinting is what will make each and everyone of us unique. As a soul we choose our character in this movie and we are setting ourselves up by choosing a society, a culture and parents (guardians) that will influence us to play our part.

So, God has set this up so we can be molded and shaped into the characters we are supposed to play in the Movie of Life. During our first years as a human being we are actually downloading life-shaping programs by observing and listening to our primary teachers - our parents (guardians), siblings, and local community. As such we are in fact being molded by the environment. We end up with certain paradigms based on what is being 'fed' into our subconscious mind. This programming is molding and shaping our character in the movie.

For more than 50 years author and speaker Bob Proctor has been looking into why some people are successful and others not. It's because of paradigms, he says. It has nothing to do with intellect or education. He says that a paradigm is a multitude of habits that are lodged in our subconscious mind. The conscious mind, on the other hand, is where our intellect resides and that's what school, parents, guardians are always having us work on - teaching us to develop our intellect, but that is not what controls our behavior. The one running the show is the subconscious mind and that is where the paradigm is. That is where the ideas are all locked up, he says. [38]

You must deposit the idea in the treasury of your subconscious mind.
- William James

Unfortunately, a lot of false believes were deposited in the treasury of our subconscious mind, Proctor says. In fact we inherit believes. We arc being conditioned while we are growing up - molded and shaped by parents, siblings, guardians and the local community. We are essentially taught the way the world works and operates by our parents and other primary teachers, but what we are taught is often what our parents were taught, which is also what their parents taught them. As we get older some wake up and realize that this truth is not so true after all. The world and our reality is not what our parents told us it was. Those who wake up see how our consciousness creates reality, and how our perception of reality is responsible for shaping our reality. We see that we are all like cells in a cosmic body and it is the conditioning that makes us different. This is what shapes us, molds us and turn us into the characters we are supposed to play in this movie.

This is how the game is set-up. We are being molded into the part we are supposed to play in the Game of Life and we don´t know it - we are unaware of the set-up. We are like actors in a movie, but we can´t re-member the part we play because it would defeat the purpose. We can´t re-member that we are God in Disguise. God has constructed a set-up where we are molded into the part we are supposed to play. How else would we be able to play our part without knowing it was a part? We must think that our world is real if the game is to work.

As souls we choose our parents, siblings and our circumstances. Why? Because they will provide the environment we need in order to create ourselves anew this time around. But then it's easy to see how your parents affect who you are, so you could say that you come as a set, rather than an actually choice per se. You see the whole cycle already happened from the infinite perspective. Your parents were cast at the same non-time that you were. We all have a soul contract - a purpose for being here and we need to play our part in the game. Without a set-up like this we would be "on to God" and realize it was all a game to experience ourselves - to define who we are - who God is. It would be difficult for us to play this game with full awareness and a complete memory of the whole set-up. We would avoid some of the pain we must go through. We wouldn't want to do it. We wouldn't choose it. Then God through us would experience less of what there is to experience in this world of duality and opposites. Our lack of awareness and memory at this stage is as such necessary.

In the setup of "this game" we are being molded step-by-step by our parents, siblings, and local community during our first six years and *beyond*, but the programs during the first six years have the biggest impact. These programs (paradigms) stick with us until we realize that they can be changed. Our understanding of the human mind has come a long way. We now see how we are run by our subconscious programming in our everyday life. Our fate is being controlled by the programs in our subconscious mind. Just a few decades ago no-one knew the power of our subconscious mind, but now we have a whole new understanding.

Why now? Why are we figuring this out now? Because it's time. We have reached that part of the cycle. We are being given yet another piece of the puzzle in re-membering who we are. We are ready to move on - to see a bigger picture of the puzzle. Some people with NDE have glimpsed part of this cycle - what is to come - what is ahead of us. They have seen what we call the future which is just another "part" further along the cycle. One example previously mentioned is Jenny Somers from the documentary *Afterlife*. While having a NDE she saw her mother die two years into the future. She explains:

I took back some of the future events my family was going to go through on Earth. I told my mother of impending death. When I woke up from the coma and saw my Mom I said: "Mom, mom you're going to die in two years". [57]

After Jenny recovered and got back home she couldn´t remember saying it. Her memories of this future event faded away, but two years later her mother died in a car accident just like Jenny said she would. We move along a cycle and we think that what is in front of us is our future, but now we are beginning to see the bigger picture and realize it´s a cycle - not a linear view with past, present and future. The memories of who we are keep surfacing and we learn (remember) that we are body, mind and soul.

Is this information new to you? Is this the first time you hear this type of information? Right now you are reading this book. How were you guided to find it? Did a friend or someone else recommend it to you, and if yes why did they decide to do that? Or maybe you bought it on the Internet? What caught your attention? Why did you decide to buy this book and read it? Where did the idea come from that this book might be of interest to you? I am telling you that the construct of your subconscious mind is part of the bigger space-time construct and that you can change the subconscious programming, but only because your part is ready for it.

Some people will never see this book or others like it. They will never hear of it, read it or know anything about the set-up of the space-time construct, the set-up of how our subconscious mind is part of the "molding and shaping process". Why? Because it is not part of their experience - it is not part of the character they play. But it´s part of your character otherwise you would never ever read this book and books like this one. Think back and see how you were guided

103

to get this book. Are you a spiritual seeker? Are you an intuitive person? Do you just know that something within creation is brewing - that something will reveal itself to you? And then you felt that this book somehow spoke out to you?

As a reader of this material you are on the inner journey to wholeness and completion of the self. You are seeking to bring your soul alive in a human body of flesh and blood. The memories of who you really are come alive - they are surfacing - they are being stirred. When this happens you will often become attracted to certain books or people, who throw a different light on ideas and values you always took for granted. Indeed the principle was mentioned years back in The Celestine Prophecy, a book (and movie) that played a major part in kicking this whole thing into shape. Maybe you will be shaken by their new thoughts - find it thought provoking, and yet strangely you are somehow attracted to it. You can´t help but read and hear more about it.

It will probably change your thinking as it did with me. Reading and speaking to other open minded people can also be helpful in this process. I remember devouring spiritual books like they were my favorite meal and "randomly" meeting people with knowledge and insight helping me to awaken the soul within even more. This is how my journey started and I do believe this is how the spiritual journey back to remembrance starts for many. Deep within you, something wants to awaken and change. Many feel this now and often this translates itself as the need for a new way of thinking.

We are living in a time of awakening, but not all will wake up. My character - my part is to spread information that will help certain characters in the play wake up. This is my soul/ sole purpose and in this chapter I am talking about how our subconscious mind sets up a certain frequency - a personal vibration - putting the Law of Attraction into work - attracting events and situations into our lives, but they seem random. There is no such thing as a random situation. There are no co-incidences. It all starts when we are growing up. These programs we 'download' as children are putting everything into motion. Our thoughts and feelings emit a certain frequency and through the Law of Vibration and Law of Attraction we can play our part and it all seems random. It ´s part of the set-up so we as souls can go through the different experiences helping us to define who we are.

If you knew ahead of time that you had to go through something painful in life you probably wouldn´t do it. As such the understanding of who you really are would be lessened. God wants to experience itself through us, but as human beings we would probably not agree to the part we are supposed to play. Hence God has set up this clever system with low brain wave activity from the time we are born to six years of age causing us to be in a hypnotic state where we have no say in it. We are being programmed to play our part. God is molding our part through the other characters in the play while we are growing up.

However - the time has come for a shift in order to move along the cycle of creation and as such we are starting to see this set-up. We start to realize that we become what we think about and what we think about is run by our subconscious mind. When we are aware of this set-up we can use techniques to alter the programming. By constantly feeding our subconscious mind with "new programs" we will set up a different vibration and attract new situations and events into our lives.

We are becoming *conscious co-creators*. This awareness is also part of the bigger plan. You wouldn´t be getting an idea to re-program your mind in order to attract new events, circumstances and people into your life if your part in the play was to be subject to your current programming and conditioning. Everything happens for a reason. There are no co-incidences and as such the question arises if we really have free will. It might seem like we have free will, but most people live in bondage subject to their subconscious programming unaware that they attract everything into their lives.

CHAPTER SIX

FREE WILL

Are we masters of our destinies? Do we have free will? Many say we do, but is this the case? The mind is a free entity that is 'forced' into a repetitive system - a never ending cycle something which will be discussed more in chapter nine. Even people in prison feel like their minds are free. How free are we really? We are continually being guided down certain avenues. Our subconscious mind is running our decision making process, but most people are not aware of this fact. We are at the mercy of the paradigms locked inside our subconscious mind.

If we have free will to do and be whatever we want why are people all over the world struggling and suffering? Pain, stress, hunger, financial worries, etc. Why do we use our free will to choose this if we don´t want it? Why don´t we pursue or dreams instead? Why do some people succeed and others not? Why don´t all succeed if we have free will? Bad luck, chance and circumstance? Is that the reason? Yes, if creation is a result of a cosmic coincidence -a random event. Then it makes sense, but evidence suggests that creation is a result of intelligent design.

How can we believe in a creator, intelligent design, and at the same time believe in free will? How does it work? If there is a creator who is in control how can we also be in control? We are like actors in a movie. We play different parts and the characters can´t 'write themselves out of the script'.

In his book *The Disappearance of the Universe* Gary R. Renard also talk about how everything was pre-programmed:

...the universe follows a script that was made in a holographic way but appears to play out in a linear manner, like a movie that has already been filmed. The whole thing has already been written, and so has your life story. [5.1]

We play the parts we have been given and it seems like we have free will. And it has to be this way. Otherwise, it would be pointless to play all the characters we have played in lifetime after lifetime. Every life has a certain destiny. It can be compared to a train going on tracks towards a destination. You are in one of the train compartments free to move around like you wish. The train passes through many different landscapes. You can choose to observe the landscape by looking out the window on the left side of the train or the right side.

The left and right sides represent the opposites. Left being the negative, pessimistic view and the right being the opposite - the positive, optimistic view. When you observe the landscape from the left side of the train you would perceive the landscape as being dull, boring and negative. If, on the other hand, you observe the landscape from the right side of the train you find it to be beautiful, uplifting and positive.

This is the law of polarity. When a situation or event comes into your life how do you deal with it? Is the glass half empty or half full? Do you choose to only see the negative in the situation or are you able to see the positive which also must be part of it? This is how I see free will. All our lives are predestined to go through certain landscapes since we all came here to experience different parts of life. But the question is how we deal with the landscape we go through. How do we handle and relate to different situations and events seemingly appearing into our lives? You may at any time choose to move from the left side of the train to the right side in every situation in your life, but you can´t make the train change tracks. As such the free will concept is part of the construct, but on a deeper level there is a destiny plan behind all our lives.

Most people go to work to earn money. Not everyone, but most. They don´t go to work because they truly love their job. I don´t think they wake up every morning saying: *Yes, another great day at work awaits me. Can´t wait to get going.* If you don´t like your job you can use your free will to quit anytime. No one is forcing you to stay. *Yes,* you might say. *I have to support my family and go to work to make a living.* Yes, we are still dependent on money with the current world model, but you don´t have to go to work if don´t like your job.

As Bob Proctor says: *We should go to work because we love it.* Instead of doing a job you don´t like you could spend time pursuing your dreams, but most people don´t do that? Why? Because a choice involves consequences. If you pursue your dream you might worry about earning enough money to get by. How will you pay your bills? Will you make it? What if you fail? Many doubt and fear the worst outcome and they stay where they are - it´s safe. No risk, but who told you it´s a risk to quit your job and pursue your dream? The programs in your subconscious mind.

We have been programmed and conditioned to think and act in a certain way since birth: *it´s better to be safe than sorry*, so we don´t pursue our dreams. Much of what we learned was based on misperceptions that are now expressed as limiting and self-sabotaging beliefs, as Bruce Lipton explains in his book *Spontaneous Evolution*. The fear in us is strong and we keep 'beating ourselves up' saying things like:

If I leave a secure job and pursue my dream I might not earn enough money and I might get into serious financial trouble. I might end up on the street.

However, if you want to pursue your dream think positive and see it vividly in your mind. Keep giving your dream attention and energy. Be around people who support you and your dream. Then you will build up courage to pursue it since you are becoming a *conscious creator*. Stay clear of negative people trying to tell you it can´t be done. They are just reinforcing the existing negative programming in your subconscious mind. Even if there is no free will, who is to say that your dreams are not already written! You'll never know if you don't try for them! It may be easier than you think; you may have a ticket reserved, but for most people this programming keep us where we are. They are strong and they were 'placed' in our subconscious mind while growing up. We were conditioned to think in a certain way. Why? It´s part of the set-up. It´s how you got your role in the game of life. You character was shaped and sculpted while you were growing up, but now your character will play a new part - a conscious co-creator.

If it´s true that this 3D world is an illusion and that we are like actors playing in a movie how would we get our part? How would it be 'handed out to us?' How could we become the character we are supposed to play? There must be a set-up to ensure we play our character. Actors in movies or on stage read the script to understand and get acquainted with their roles - with their characters. It´s the same with the soul. As souls we are assigned the roles we are to play. As such we need an environment than can produce a character matching what we need to go through this time around. And remember, a choice to suffer somewhat in the beginning from the over view is just a necessary evil and only a small section of your greater journey. Very different from where we are, all our lives have been spent in the premise paying in (pain = pay in). So we see it as everything.

We can't see the light at the end of the tunnel, the bigger picture, so we tend to lose hope. However, when you understand the cycle, you can look forwards again. We are assigned our parents, the time period, Earth etc. and off we go to create ourselves anew once again. Nothing is a coincidence, so in a way we 'read the script and our part' before we are born. Many spiritual teachers, like my friend Bryan de Flores, talk about how we enter into soul contracts - soul charts before we 'arrive' here on Earth. These contracts would be the equivalent to how an actor reads the script for a movie.

When we are born we forget, but the link to our soul contract is intact through our intuition. It 'knows the script' and the parts you are supposed to play, but as we grow up we have no clue. We forget in order to re-member. So, how would The Mind make sure you, as a soul using a human body, would play your part? By letting the external word and the environment you grow up in program you - by conditioning you from the day you are born in order for the subconscious mind to 'run the show.' If we don´t know that the subconscious mind is 'running the show' we think we have free will. In a way our minds are trapped in the space-time construct system via the body, which is not real. It's a vehicle we use to navigate the system. You could say that we are stuck in the carriage on a ride. We feel that we are in control, but are we really?

In theory you reactions and actions are your own, but then the ride takes you down certain avenues. You are guided into experiencing certain situations causing pain or pleasure. Certain situations will be painful and we suffer. It might be a stressful divorce, losing a job, being sick for a long time and so on. If you had free will and complete control why would you want these things to happen to you? They come into your life because it´s part of the Divine Plan so you can get the experience you need this time around. Being by doing. These situations are 'drawn' into your life by what you vibrate out as a frequency to the Universe - Law of Vibration setting up the Law of Attraction. This frequency is set up by what you think and feel which is set-up by your subconscious mind which has been programmed since birth. In a way we are like marionettes, but since we are God in Disguise we are guiding ourselves. We are pulling the strings. The Higher Self (the soul) is doing the pulling. The Higher Self knows which experience we need this time around.

Our experience is sent to us by God through this set-up of vibration and attraction before we are consciously aware of it. What you experience in every moment is as such pre-sent to you. It is a gift - a present - given from God (The Higher Self) so we can re-member who we are. This gift - this present - is about being in the present - in the now and embracing what we experience - both "good and bad". How does this Higher Self guidance relate to the subconscious mind? Isn´t the subconscious mind in control? There is a link between the two.

What you have is a higher, wiser part of you always giving you information in the form of an inner feeling or certainty. We call it *intuition* (inner tuition). It knows why you are here and which part you are to play this time around. It guides you down certain avenues.

Intuition can be defined as:

- *direct perception of truth, fact, etc., independent of any reasoning process*
- *knowledge gained not through the reasoning process or the five senses.*

In other words intuition *is not a conscious process.* There is no step-by-step procedure using logic and reasoning involved. The word *intuition* comes from the Latin word *intueri* which is usually translated as to look inside. [39]

Inside being the inner feeling - the gut feeling. Intuition is looking inside. We can access our subconscious mind through our intuition and this is the link between the two. The guiding is very subtle. It seems like our own choices, but research shows that we are conscious of only 3% of our cognitive activity. Most of our decisions, actions and behavior depend on the 97% of the brain activity that goes beyond our conscious awareness. It´s run by our subconscious mind. It´s autonomic - automatic - habits go on automatic pilot. In other words the subconscious mind runs the show. [36]

Ultimately your subconscious programming is the one 'in charge' and this was set-up by The Mind. Our subconscious mind is our connection to The Mind. One way to illustrate this is found in the book *Krishna: The Man and His Philosophy* written by spiritual teacher Osho:

The conscious is the superficial part of the mind which is lighted, and below it lies the unconscious buried in the dark. Then below the unconscious lies the collective unconscious, and at the bottom lies the cosmic unconscious – which is the mind of the entire universe, which is the total mind, the universal mind. [40]

We are, in other words, linked to The Cosmic Mind of God through our subconscious mind and by paying attention to our intuition we can access it. So, intuition and the subconscious mind are interlinked. In our world today we have lost touch with our intuition. We don´t pay attention to the inner voice (feeling) and as such we are unconsciously creating our reality. No awareness. When we wake up and listen to our intuition we become aware of The Plan - our part in this game - which character we chose to play in the movie. We become conscious co-creators. You are here on a mission - you have a soul contract to complete and The Mind is guiding you. The Mind (God) also being your Higher Self - your intuition.

For many years I was going on autopilot. A typical day

would go something like this: 05:45 - alarm clock goes off - time to get up. 05:45-06:30 - *shower, breakfast while reading the newspaper - off to work.* 06:30-08:00 - *driving to work - commuting for an hour and 30 minutes while listening to news updates on the radio.* 08:00-16:30 - *work.* 16:30-18:00 - *driving back home and listening to more news updates.* 18:00-21:00 - *Dinner, kids activities, exercise.* 21:00-23:00 - *relaxing and watching TV (incl. news updates) and checking work e-mail.* 23:00 - *go to bed* only to wake up the next morning doing the same schedule all over again.

I didn´t pay any attention to my intuition. I was just reacting to the outside world and my conscious mind was constantly busy sorting out all the impression as the day went by. After years of this "auto-piloting" I finally woke up and become aware. I started to listen to my thoughts and pay attention to my intuition and I realized that I am part of something bigger. This was my turning point.

When we don´t see the bigger picture it seems like we have free will. Life seems like a string of co-incidences and we only see the obvious outcomes - the direct effect of a cause. If you put your hand on a hot stove you know you will burn yourself. We see the consequences of the laws of physics and the laws of man, but we don´t see the consequences of the "other laws" in action. Laws like the law of vibration, the law of attraction and the law of cause and effect dealing with our thoughts, feelings and vibrations. We also pay little attention to our intuition and as such we miss out on the bigger picture.

From birth we are being conditioned to interpret our experiences in a certain way, and this determines how we react to them. We don´t see how the programming is running our lives. It was set-up this way in order for the game to work. When we are born our brain waves are in Theta and Delta mode. As previously mentioned these brainwave frequencies define a brain state known as hypnotic trance - the same neural state that hypnotherapists use to directly download new behaviors into the subconscious minds of their clients. [37]

As such we are being molded and shaped, by the chosen external environment - parents (guardians), siblings, local community, into the part we are supposed to play. Our subconscious mind is being given whatever we need to mold into the chosen character. In that sense we are in bondage because what we experience is the prison of our own conditioning. When we are ignorant of how this game is set-up we get triggered by other people and circumstances and the outcome is given. It is easy to predict. We go through anger, bitterness, guilt and many other so-called bad/negative emotions, and we don´t see how this is part of what we must go through in order to gain experiences as a soul. We need the duality - the polarity that this 3D world has to offer. It´s part of the game we play. What comes into our lives is not a co-incidence. So, do we have any freedom at all? What would freedom be? Deepak Chopra defines freedom as this:

Freedom is the experiential knowledge of our true nature, which is already free. It comes from finding out that our real essence is the joyful field of infinite consciousness that animates all of creation. To have the experience of our real essence is just to be. Then we are free. In this state of freedom, we understand that life is the meaningful coexistence of all opposite values. We may experience happiness or we may experience pain and suffering, but we do not get attached to pleasure and we do not recoil in fear of pain. In freedom, we even lose our fear of death, because the belief in mortality is just a spell that we have cast upon ourselves.

Behind the mask of mortality is the field of immortality. The real you is immortal; it is beyond birth and death. The real you is not your ego, which is time-bound; it is your spirit, which is timeless. When you know that, when you identify with your spirit, you are free of every limitation, including the limitation that you are a person trapped inside a body for the span of a lifetime. You are the source of both body and mind, and you are not touched by this world of change because you know that you are the unchanging essence of pure consciousness itself. [41]

But then what is freedom? Being all alone outside of a construct with nothing to do? Is that freedom? We are not our body. We are spiritual beings having a physical experience in this 3D world. The body is the vehicle we use to create and experience - to do in order to *be*. As such we have been given different roles to play. We are like actors in a movie and when we realize this we see that even the painful moments in our lives were part of The Plan to learn and understand which is actually to re-member who we really are. Earth is the playground, but it´s not real. This world we think we touch and taste is not real, but it sure feels real. You can understand it's a construct of mind like a dream, but then even when you are in a dream you go along with it, accept it. It's very hard to feel that the world is not real when you are in it.

That is a realization that comes after impeccable logical examination, and even when you know it's not physical you still feel physical. You can understand that your life is run by your subconscious mind, but still you will always feel like you are in charge of what happens in your life and if something bad happens we call it bad luck. In the book *I Am That: Talks with Sri Nisargadatta Maharaj* there is a question and answer section about free will. Below is an excerpt. Q stands for questioner and M stands for Sri Nisargadatta Maharaj:

Q: Surely, I am not the master of what happens. It's slave rather.
M: Be neither master, nor slave. Stand aloof.

Q: Does it imply avoidance of action?
M: You cannot avoid action. It happens, like everything else.

Q: My actions, surely, I can control.
M: Try. You will soon see that you do what you must.

Q: I can act according to my will.
M: You know your will only after you have acted.

Q: I remember my desires, the choices made, the decisions taken and act accordingly.
M: Then your memory decides, not you.

Q: Where do I come in?
M: You make it possible by giving it attention.

Q: Is there no such thing as free will? Am I not free to desire?
M: Oh no. You are compelled to desire. In Hinduism the very idea of free will is non-existent, so there is no word for it. Will is commitment, fixation, and bondage.

Q: I am free to choose my limitations.
M: You must be free first. To be free in the world you must be free of the world. Otherwise your past decides for you and your future. Between what had happened and what must happen you are caught. Call it destiny or karma, but never—freedom. First return to your true being and then act from the heart of love. [42]

Yes, to be free *in* the world we must first be free *of* the world.

> *As you surrender the hold that the illusions of your psyche have created as your surroundings, your life, your everything; all those illusions will no longer govern you. This is true freedom and where true creation can begin from a point of inner power and connection in unison with your co-creators.* [30]

You are like a carriage on rails and even when you realize this you still feel free because you always feel free in mind. However, nothing is really random. There are no coincidences. We attract events, people and circumstances into our lives with what we are thinking and feeling, but where does the thinking and feeling come from? Our subconscious mind. It sets up the frequency we emit and put the Law of Vibration and Attraction into motion. Hence we attract situations into our lives without being aware of it. We are here to play our part - we are God in Disguise, but most people don´t re-member. We ignore our intuition, but once we start to pay attention to it we will begin to understand that we truly are God in Disguise and life takes on a new meaning. You will start to re-member and your character will now be able to be a conscious creator because your will is God´s will. You return to your true being and then act from your heart like Sri Nisargadatta Maharaj talks about.

When we start to re-member we realize that we can change the programming of our subconscious mind and there are many methods available. Prof. Lipton has listed many great resources on his website (http://brucelipton.com/resources). He calls these resources *Belief Change and Energy Psychology Modalities*

If we are in a movie and we play a certain part which has been molded by our subconscious programming why are we now given the tools to change that programming? Why would The Mind "let us" find out about the set-up? Because it is part of the movie. It´s part of the cycle. We are supposed to re-member who we are and now we can become conscious co-creators. We are moving along the cycle and now we can create Heaven on Earth. This is The Shift many talk about. It is upon us.

By meditating and going deep inside - into stillness we can connect with The Mind and we´ll see that our individual impulse of growth is identical with that of the Mind. The Mind never really develops. It never needs to learn or understand or evolve. The Mind knows it all, but it is lacking experience of this knowing - of this potential. The greatest desire of The Mind is to create and experience through each and everyone of us in order to define itself - to be. *Being by doing.*

When you move into stillness and get in touch with your intuition you will see that your desires and the will of God are the same.

Intuition = Latin word intueri = to look inside

This lifetime is about becoming a conscious co-creator. To wake up and create for yourself *and others.* Creation is about *giving.* Giving of your uniqueness to the world. All the people on this planet are just mirrors of your Self. There is only one of us here. When you create and give you are giving to yourself and in that you are experiencing how it feels to be the one who creates and gives and also how it feels to be the recipient of the gift. This is why we need interaction with other people, places and events. Earth and every human being are part of the space-time construct so we can experience in order to be.

It´s only through our relationship with other people, places, and events that we can exist in this space-time construct. If there were no people, no events and no places how could you know yourself? No mirror - no reflection. You have come to Earth because the Earth and the people here are part of the space-time construct and they provide the tools you need to re-member who you are, the inter-act-I-on. Creation, experience and interaction with others are tools to aid in this dis-covery.

Who You Are is who you create yourself to be in relationship to all the rest of it.
- Neal Donald Walsh

Without the 'mirrors'- the others - without the construct you are nothing, No Thing, but you are here to create and experience so No Thing can be Some Thing - Every Thing.

And in that you need interaction with other people, places and events. Hence the space-time construct.

As souls we use the human body to create. The human body is electromagnetic. The brain and the heart produce powerful electromagnetic energy. What we think and feel is setting up what we experience in our lives. What we give energy and focus to is what we attract into our lives. People, events and places seem to come into our lives by co-incidence, but they do not. We draw them into our lives with what we think and feel, and since the subconscious mind is running the show it sets it up. Energy can become matter. Einstein proved this with his $e=mc^2$. Thoughts and feelings are energy. They are the tools we use to create, but since we are subject to how we have been conditioned most people are not aware of these incredible tools. They are gifts and part of the set-up.

CHAPTER SEVEN

TOOLS FOR CREATION

In 1956 Earl Nightingale recorded *The Strangest Secret* - an audio recording that has changed the lives of millions of people all over the world. Today, several decades later, The Strangest Secret remains one of the most powerful and influential messages ever recorded. It continues to transform the lives of everyone who hears it. Why? What is it all about? It´s about how *We Become What We Think About*. Earl Nightingale grew up as child in the Depression-era. He was hungry for knowledge and he was constantly searching for the answer to the following question:

How can a person, starting from scratch, who has no particular advantage in the world, reach the goals that he feels are important to him, and by so doing, make a major contribution to others?

He had a burning desire to find the answer and coupled with his natural curiosity about the world and its workings it spurred him to become one of the world's foremost experts on success and what makes people successful. Where did this burning desire come from? It came from The Mind. He wanted to help people and by helping people he was giving. Giving of ourselves is what God wants. Sharing is caring and since we are all One we should all share with one another. The famous speaker and author Bob Proctor has on many occasions praised Earl Nightingale and his incredible commitment to share with other people - to help other people. Earl lived by this statement: *What I want for myself I want for everyone*. Earl became Bob´s mentor and they worked together for some years and Bob adopted the same statement. He too started living by this statement. Both became successful beyond their wildest dreams. Why? They were aligned with God´s will. Create and give. We are here to create for ourselves *and others*.

Earl´s search for the answer to what makes people successful came to him after years of contemplating this question. When reading Napoleon Hill´s book *Think &Grow Rich* he found the answer: *We Become What We Think About.* Napoleon Hill published his book in 1937 after 20 years of research on what makes people successful. He had been engaged by Andrew Carnegie, one of the richest man in the world at that time, to do this research. Before Mr. Hill started his research Mr. Carnegie delivered a speech to him saying the following:

Let me call your attention to a great power which is under your control. A power that is greater than poverty, greater than the lack of education, greater than all of your fears and superstitions combined. It is the power to take possession of your mind and direct it to whatever ends you must desire. This profound power is the gift of the Creator and it must have been considered the greatest of all of his gifts to man, because it is the only thing over which man has the complete and unchallengeable right of control and direction. When you speak of your poverty and lack of education you are simple directing your mind power to attract these undesirable circumstances, because it is true that whatever the mind feeds upon the mind attracts to you.

Everyone comes to the Earth plane blessed with the privilege of controlling his mind power and directing it to whatever ends he may choose. But, everyone brings with them at birth the equivalent of two sealed envelopes - One of which is clearly labeled: The riches you may enjoy if you take possession of your own mind and direct it to ends of your own choice. And the other is labeled: The penalties you must pay if you neglect to take possession of your mind and direct it. Let me reveal to you the content of those two sealed envelopes.

In the one labeled riches is this list of blessing:

1. Sound health
2. Peace of Mind
3. A Labor of Love of your own choice
4. Freedom from Fear and Worry
5. A positive mental attitude
6. Material riches of your own choice and quantity

In the sealed envelope labeled Penalties is this list of prices one must pay for neglecting to take possession of one's own mind:

1. Ill health
2. Fear and worry
3. Indecision and Doubt
4. Frustration and Discouragement throughout life
5. Poverty and Want
6. A whole flock of evils consisting of envy, greed, jealousy, anger, hatred and superstition [43]

Napoleon Hill found this to be true when he interviewed a wide range of successful people during his research - people like Thomas Edison and Henry Ford. When Earl Nightingale came across Mr. Hill´s work in *Think & Grow Rich* he found the answer to his question: *how can anyone who has no particular advantage in the world reach the goals that he feels are important to him, and by so doing, make a major contribution to others?*

The answer was and still is: *whatever the mind feeds upon the mind attract*s. In Earl´s *The Strangest Secret* he explains this by comparing the human mind with that of a farmer's land. He says:

Suppose a farmer has some land. And it is good fertile land. The land gives the farmer a choice. He may plant in that land whatever he chooses. The land doesn't care what is planted. It's up to the farmer to make the decision. Remember we are comparing the human mind to the farmers land because, the mind, like the land, doesn't care what you plant in it. It will return what you plant, but it doesn't care what you plant. Let's say that the farmer has two seeds in his hand - one a seed of corn, the other is nightshade, a deadly poison. He digs two little holes in the earth and he plants both seeds, one corn, the other nightshade. He covers up the holes, waters, and takes care of the land. What will happen? Invariably, the land will return what is planted. As it is written in the Bible, "As you sow, so shall you reap." Remember, the land doesn't care. It will return poison in just as wonderful abundance as it will corn. So up come the two plants - one corn, one poison. The human mind is far more fertile, far more incredible and mysterious than the land, but it works the same way. It does not care what we plant ... success ... or failure. A concrete, worthwhile goal ... or confusion, misunderstanding, fear, anxiety, and so on. But what we plant it must return to us. [44]

In other words *we become what we think about.* This is how The Mind of God has set the construct up. We are souls using a human body as a vehicle to create, explore, express and experience the un-manifested potential of The Mind of God. As such God is always acting through us and hence we are conscious, thinking, feeling energy beings. The world we live in is electromagnetic. We are energy. Our thoughts and feelings are energy. Hence we can attract into our lives whatever we think about and whatever we feel. This sets up a vibration which is sent into the ether - into the universe created by The Mind. The Law of Vibration states that everything within this Universe moves and vibrates - everything is vibrating at one speed or another. Nothing rests. This is true within the created construct of space and time.

Since All is Mind all that ever moves is perspective. There is actually no true movement as there is no real physical element. Movement is shifting perspective in The Mind. Within our Universe there is only perceived movement. Everything you see around you is vibrating at one frequency or another, and so are you. Your frequency is different from other things in the Universe - so it seems like you are separated from what you see around you - people, animals, plants, trees and so on, but you are not. You are in fact living in an ocean of energy - we all are. This is part of the set up. Part of the program.

David Icke is a former professional football player, BBC sports journalist, author and lecturer who believes that we are all part of a gigantic, advanced super hologram. He says that this super hologram consists of vibrations that have been decoded to form an illusory world that we think we are experiencing as reality. He compares it to a computer. A computer reads and decodes software and decodes the wireless Internet on your computer. Icke says that in the same way the information (vibrations) we decode from the super hologram is a ready-made world. The hologram sends this information to the body's DNA as frequencies and this is decoded by our five senses as a solid reality in three dimensions, but it is actually a hologram:

The Prime state of everything is vibrational so that is where the game is played.
- David Icke

This is the set-up. The Mind - God - creates a playground in the finite and lay down the ground rules using Universal Laws like the Law of Vibration to 'fool us' into believing that the reality we see is actually real. God - The Mind was here first and then everything else 'kicks in' in order to define and experience the potential of The Mind. Since experience is linear we keep on rolling along in the space-time construct

125

thinking it's real. The game is set up to be played at the vibrational level so this is where you have to start. But how?

The human body is electromagnetic. We are electrical and magnetic beings. People with heart problems have had their hearts "restarted" with an electrical heart starter. Why? Because the heart is electrical. The same with the brain. When you are thinking you are emitting electrical signals. In addition, both the heart and the brain emit magnetic signals. The research company HearthMath has been researching electromagnetic fields from the brain and heart for many years.

Their findings show that the human heart generates the strongest electromagnetic field in the body, far greater than the brain. It is approximately 60 times more powerful electrically, and up to 5,000 times more powerful magnetically than the brain.[45] In other words your thoughts and feelings are powerful. These electromagnetic signals are what we vibrate out. What you send out into the ether - to The Mind is what you think and feel. Since the heart generates the strongest electromagnetic field in the body being passionate about something is what will set up the strongest vibration.

Within this space-time construct everything consists of atoms. Scientists know that atoms can be altered if the electrical or magnetic fields surrounding them changes. The heart is capable of doing both and this make you realize how much power you actually have to influence your 3D reality. What you think and feel will set up The Law of Vibration which again sets up the Law of Attraction. As such the part you play in this Game of Life will attract to it whatever it needs in order to play out its character - events, places, people. However, we don't see this. We are unaware of the strong programming we have been subject to and how the subconscious mind runs the show by setting up our frequency, but this is now changing.

The greatest revolution in our generation is that of human beings, who by changing the inner attitude of their minds can change the outer aspects of their lives. [46]
- Marilyn Ferguson

In her book *We Live Forever* P.M.H. Atwater describes how our thoughts form as shapes in the ether. She could see the power of thoughts when she experienced being dead. In her first near-death experience she could see 'blobs' forming in the air around her. She didn´t know what else to call these strange shapes. They were dark grey, misshapen things that looked link ink blots. When she died the second time she realized that the gray blobs she had witnessed during her first near-death experience were *raw thought substances*, unshaped because they lacked the focus she could have provided. She discovered that *thoughts really are things* - that thinking a thought produces the energy and the substance needed for it to exist by itself. Even though most thoughts are short-lived those we put effort into, focus on, or think intensely about become the climate or atmosphere we live in. [5] She could see what Einstein put forth in his formula $e=mc^2$. Energy can become matter and matter can become energy. Thoughts are electromagnetic and thus energy. However it requires *a lot* of energy for it to become matter. This is why Atwater said the blots she saw were unshaped - they lacked focus - they lacked energy. If we keep thinking the same thought over and over and over again it will become matter.

What we send out is what is coming back. However, since most people are programmed with limiting and self-sabotaging beliefs this is what is being broadcasted into the Universe and coming back. We are consciously not aware of it. It goes unnoticed so the events and situations coming into our lives seem random. BUT, this is changing now. We are becoming conscious co-creator. We realize that what we constantly think about will become matter which is our reality. Thoughts do become things as Neal Donald Walsch also talks about in *Conversations with God*:

Thought is pure energy…..All thoughts congeal; all thoughts meet other thoughts, criss-crossing in an incredible maze of energy, forming an ever-changing pattern of unspeakable beauty and unbelievable complexity. Like energy attracts like energy—forming (to use simple words) "clumps" of energy of like kind. When enough similar "clumps" criss-cross each other—run into each other—they "stick to" each other (to use another simple term). It takes an incomprehensibly huge amount of similar energy "sticking together," thusly, to form matter. But matter will form out of pure energy. In fact, that is the only way it can form. Once energy becomes matter, it remains matter for a very long time—unless its construction is disrupted by an opposing, or dissimilar, form of energy. This dissimilar energy, acting upon matter, actually dismembers the matter, releasing the raw energy of which it was composed. [4]

The atomic bomb was proof that Einstein´s equation is correct. When the atom was split matter became raw energy. As such energy can also become matter and since the subconscious mind runs the show we have to be aware of what we think. What we give our thoughts to will become matter - will become our reality. Being passionate about something will make it easier for you to vibrate out what you want to happen. When you are passionate about something, when you involve the heart, you automatically think about it all the time. It occupies you. It consumes you. It´s like being in love. You don´t need a reminder telling you you´re in love. You think about the one you are in love with 24-7.

Likewise, when you become passionate about an idea you

saturate all your cells with that passion. You are tapping into your soul instead of just reacting and letting the subconscious mind run the show. A reaction is an action you have taken before (re-action), but why do we act/react in the same manner every time we encounter a certain situation? It's because of paradigms - the programs stored in our subconscious mind. Whatever paradigm is stored there will determine the action we take. The paradigm is the truth we hold about something and we let this run our actions.

However, when you are passionate about something you are tapping into your soul and not into your subconscious mind. You are 'out of your mind' since you are not letting the programs dictate your actions. You respond rather than react. You are setting up your home frequency (soul) rather than your personal frequency (mind). Passion comes from within and is pure. It is *focused* energy and as such you create matter which is actually creating your own reality. *E*-motion is *energy* in motion. Being passionate about something will move energy and when you move enough energy, you create matter. Matter is energy - e=mc^2 as Einstein dis-covered. As such, situations and events come into our lives for a purpose - they are drawn in to provide the reality we want to experience as souls - as God in Disguise. We were involved in creating them. As Jill Mara says in *Keys to Soul Evolution*:

All parties were equally involved in the creation of the event as it came about. All must take full responsibility for their part in its creation. Nothing was done to anyone. They each attracted the occurrence into their experience so that their soul can grow. How else would you know what needs attention unless you present it in a way that it will be surely noticed? [30]

We (God) create our own reality moving energy into matter, but since most people don't know about the set-up life seems random. We really become what we think about. Our purpose is *to do* in order *to be*. We are God in Disguise using the human body as a vibrating tower. You are emitting a certain frequency right now while reading this book. You are always emitting a certain frequency. This will cause you to attract certain events, places and people into your life, but what is setting up the particular frequency you emit at any given time?

The answer is your thoughts and feelings run by your subconscious mind which has been conditioned in order for the body (the soul) to play a certain part in this game - in this movie. In truth we are asking for certain events and circumstances to come into our lives in order for the soul to grow (re-member) and in that brighten the representation of All That Is. All That Is is asking for this experience through us, but what about people born in poverty, suffering and pain? Why does God include such 'bad' experiences in the game? Why the hurt, the pain, the suffering?
Nothing is a coincidence, but this is hard to accept when we talk about suffering, but this too is part of the soul contract - what some souls come here to experience. As soul aspects representing God we experience the full scale of e-motions - from pain to pleasure. This time around some souls have chosen more pain than others. As a soul we know we can direct our minds to whatever ends we want - we can influence our experience with what we think and feel. However, after we are born we forget and we don´t know the power of thoughts and feelings.

As human beings we are influenced and conditioned to think and feel according to what the circumstances show us. If you are born in poverty you will get more of the same because this is what you see. Poverty is what your mind is focused on - this is what you give energy to. This is what you let into your subconscious mind resulting in a vibration attracting more of the same. It seems like a vicious circle, but some souls choose this experience because it will give them what they need in order to evolve - to re-member.

We live in a time of awakening and now we realize the power we possess in order to change what we attract into our lives. We are starting to see the set-up. When we know the set-up we can change our reality with what we think and feel. We can start making the changes we want to see, but then again - where does your thoughts come from? Ultimately from God because God is within all of us wanting to create, experience and bring its potential out into the world. When you *get* an idea to change your thinking your character in the play is ready for this new path. It's like being called on stage, it's your cue! Meaning that the construct is now changing into a format where you can excel and at the same time as you become ready, as you are waking.

It too is part of the overall set-up, because it means you are re-membering. Everyone who realizes that we create our own reality with what we think and feel is starting to re-member who they really are. We are all moving along the cycle of time - putting the puzzle together and now we have discovered yet another piece. It seems like it has been hidden from us and now it is appearing. We don´t have to suffer anymore - no more pain and struggling. More people realize the power within - the power to create our own reality using our thoughts and feelings no matter what the circumstances are and they are re-minding others.

One example is Legson Kayira who went from being illiterate and living in poverty in a small village in Africa to studying political science, becoming a professor at the University of Cambridge in England and a recognized author. Despite being unable to read and write and having no money, he nevertheless did what most people consider impossible. He was able to follow his inner voice, his dream, his flame and he changed his life for the better. He showed the world it could be done. No matter what type of circumstances you have in your life you can change them as Legson did. The inner voice he heard - the passion, the flame that was ignited, was God expressing Himself through Legson.

You are not the victim of your circumstances, but the Master of them.
- Legson Kayira

You have the power within you as Wallace D. Wattles, Andrew Carnegie, Napoleon Hill, Earl Nightingale and Legson Kayira discovered. It is the unlimited, un-manifested potential of The Mind. It is always there wanting to get out and it´s strange that so few people have discovered this power. The title of Mr. Nightingale´s audio recording - The Strangest Secret - is as such a fitting one, he explains:

Why do I say it's strange, and why do I call it a secret? Actually, it is not a secret at all. It was first promulgated by some of the earliest wise men, and it appears again and again throughout the Bible. But very few people have learned it or understand it. That's why it's strange, and why for some equally strange reason it virtually remains a secret. [44]

We reap what we sow. It has been the key message in the Bible and other scriptures for millenniums and still we miss it. Steve explains "we reap what we sow" as that the character will fulfill his role or he is not the character. His actions and who he is are One. So, if you are a baddy, you will get your comeuppance, it's just a matter of time. We are here to express the potential of The One Mind and a space-time construct has been put into play for us to do that. Our bodies are the vehicles we use to attract any type of experience we want into our lives. What we send out comes back and if your vibration is low and influenced by fear you will attract more of that into your life. Fear is just in our minds. We let the outside, external world influence us and as such it is setting up our vibrations.

You can at any time decide what should enter your mind. Do you really need to watch the news every day? Do you really need to read the tabloids every day? Most news coverage is negative. Why is that? Why do we watch and read something that is negative most of the time? No wonder researchers tell us that 70% of our thoughts are negative. We all have the ability to consider whether or not something should enter into our minds - as inspirational speaker Anthony Robbins says: *You must guard the entrance to your mind.* Whatever you allow into your conscious mind will ultimately end up in your subconscious thoughts, and the more feeling you devote to such thoughts, the greater the impact on your subconscious mind. We live inside a thinking Universe, all part of The Mind. We create our own world on the basis of our thoughts and feelings, therefore it is important to be aware of what we allow into our minds. In his book *Think & Grow Rich* Napoleon Hill talks about the subconscious mind and control:

Nature has so built man that he has ABSOLUTE CONTROL over the material which reaches his subconscious mind, through his five senses, although this is not meant to be construed as a statement that man always EXERCISES this control. In the great majority of instances, he does NOT exercise it, which explains why so many people go through life in poverty. [19]

If your mind has been exposed to a vast amount of negative information, then guarding the door to your mind to stop further influence will be imperative. To stop further negative information reaching our subconscious minds we must first realize the negative impact it has. Too many people let negative news; images, videos etc. slip into their minds without realizing the impact. Such an uncritical attitude about what the outer world feeds us can quickly result in negativity and fear sneaking into our minds. The impact is much stronger from the time we are born until six years of age since there is no conscious filter in place. As such we need to pay attention to what our children are exposed to. Even though as adults we have a conscious filter negative news and information will sneak into our subconscious mind. If you watch negative news everyday *it will* influence you. Far too many people allow the outside world to dictate their reality, but then again if you are God in Disguise then God is allowing your character to be ignorant about the set-up. Since you are reading this book your character is no longer ignorant. You are ready to be a conscious co-creator or maybe you already are. Yes, letting the negative information from the outside world sneak into our subconscious mind will set-up a low vibration. This will draw what we consider to be negative events and people into our lives. It´s part of the set-up for the characters we play. Each of us comes to the Earth plane to re-member who we are and we do this by creating and experiencing. We experience the highs and lows - like being on a roller coaster.

Only if you have been in the deepest valley, can you ever know how magnificent it is to be on the highest mountain.
- Richard M. Nixon

It is the duality - polarity world in play. Events and situations in your life will seem as bad/good luck or coincidence when you don´t re-member who you are, but once you re-member you see a purpose to everything you have experienced - both the 'good' and the 'bad.'

DYING EMPTY

In waking up you start tapping into the essence of who you really are. The flame inside ignites. It´s actually there all the time, but more in the form of tiny sparks that needs to come to live.

Make the most of yourself by fanning the tiny, inner sparks of possibility into flames of achievement.
- Foster C McClellan

We have forgotten who we are and why we came here. As such we are not conscious of these inner sparks ready to turn into flames of achievement. However, the day you wake up and know that you are God in Disguise - a point of consciousness of The Mind - the sparks turns into a flame that burns like never before. You can feel the passion inside. You are all excited and want to create and express your uniqueness and let it out into the physical world. The potential within is manifesting into the physical world - the un-manifested becomes manifested.

On this grand cycle of creation many people have gone through life without being conscious of these inner sparks of possibility. As such they die full - full of hopes, ideas, dreams and uniqueness that never got out. It stayed inside as a potential never being realized and manifested in the physical world. It was part of the puzzle too. They served their purpose so others will realize that dying *empty* is the way to go - not dying full. It is all about letting all the talents, dreams and ideas out - to express the Source within and become a *conscious co-creator.* Now is the time to re-member and get in touch with the Source within and let it all out. Most people throughout history have not done this. It´s like all this incredible power and potential is clogged up inside. It wants to get out, but we stop it.

I want to share a symbolic illustration I received on how the un-manifested potential always wants to get out into the physical, finite world through us. But first I will describe what happened prior to receiving it. This illustration came to me as an image in my mind while walking in nature. Walking in nature connects us with The Cosmic Mind and we become more receptive. I didn´t know this, but I was guided to information helping me understand how it works. Since my interest for the spiritual started many years ago I have been drawn to different people, spiritual books, movies, videos and information to give me a better insight of creation. I was also drawn to the importance of being in contact with nature and have direct contact with Mother Earth by walking barefoot. Walking barefoot connect us to The Mind and the field of Universal Consciousness. We can more easily tap into The Mind of God. How? The Earth is shielded with a big electromagnetic field. We live inside this field on planet Earth. When we are in direct contact with the Earth we are also in contact with this field. Prior to receiving the symbolic illustration I was drawn to the work of Clinton Ober, Dr. Stephen T. Sinatra and Martin Zucker.

In 2010 they published their book *Earthing* explaining the health benefits of being in physical contact with Mother Earth by either going barefoot or using an earthing bed sheet or pad to stay grounded. After reading their book I was convinced of the health benefits of being in contact with Mother Earth. I started walking barefoot in nature and also launched a web site *www.EarthPower.no* informing others about these benefits. While doing my barefoot walks in nature I would start to receive images of how I could explain my version of creation to other people. I would be more alert in my thinking and I would receive clear pictures in my mind of the symbols I could use in my work. At about the same time I was also drawn to the work of Lee Carrol. He channels an energy entity by the name of Kryon and on the topic of magnetic fields and Earth he says:

Magnetic fields are very significant to your biology! In addition, magnetic fields can (and do) affect your spiritual consciousness. The magnetic field of your planet is necessary for your biological health, and is fine tuned to fit within your spiritual scheme. The magnetic field of your planet was carefully placed for your health - and your lessons. Look around you. What other planets do you find with magnetic fields? [Not just in your solar system]. It is not a natural occurring force. It was placed purposefully and carefully. You have not been able to leave your planet far enough or long enough to realize this fact, but when you do, you must carry a field with you to continue sanity and health, and it must be correct. This is basic for humans. If you find another planet with a magnetic field, it is a prime suspect for biological life, or its arrival in the future, or a 'marker' that there used to be life there. No matter what the actual biology of the life form, it will have to be polarized to have a spiritual significance. [47]

In other words the electromagnetic field of our planet is part of the space-time construct. It is set-up by The Mind and being in contact with this field will help us connect with Universal Consciousness - with The Mind. I now understood why I had been receiving images I could use in my talks and in my writing when explaining my version of creation. As human beings we are electromagnetic by nature and when being in contact with the electromagnetic field of Mother Earth it will alter our behavior, emotions and our ability to think. As Kryon says; *it affects our spiritual consciousness.*

One day while walking barefoot in nature a picture of a water hose appeared in my mind. It showed me how humans stop the incredible potential of God within us to get out into the world - to manifest in the physical. Let me explain: Picture a water hose. One end leads to the water tap and in the other end there is a nozzle (or pistol) where you can adjust the amount of water flowing out of the hose. You can also close it completely to prevent any water from coming out. When turning on the water we have access to an unlimited water supply. We just turn the tap and we let the water flow freely through the hose, through the nozzle and out into our garden or plants or other things we need to water. Humans are like water hoses. You are unique and the nozzle represents the uniqueness in you.

We are all here to express the potential of The Mind - to let the potential out - to let it flow freely through us and into the world. This is creation. When we become passionate about an idea it is the potential of The Mind wanting to get out. It flows through us, we become conscious of the idea, we think about it and we start to manifest it through whom we are. We let it out into the world and it becomes Some Thing in the finite world. It manifests. Mission completed. We let the potential flow through us like the water in the water hose and whatever goes through us also sticks to us.

The more you give the more you get. Givers gain. If you want more money in your life - give money. There is an abundance of it and it will flow freely through you as long as you don´t close the nozzle. If you want more love - give love. The potential is always there wanting an outlet and if you open yourself up - open up your nozzle - it can flow freely through you and you will get more to give. The "water tap" is always open and as such you have access to abundance. Sadly, most people don´t do this. They close the nozzle completely and the water can´t get out. It wants to get out, but we stop the free flowing. Why? Because of FEAR. We have closed the nozzle with fear. We are afraid to be who we really are and let the potential we have inside flow freely into the world. We are afraid to go after our dreams. What if we fail? What would family members, friends, colleagues and neighbors think if we started pursuing our ideas and dreams? No, we can´t do that. It´s better to *conform* and do what the masses do. It is safe. We know what we have.

A bird in the hand is better than two in the bush.
It´s better to be safe than sorry.

Due to fear we think it´s better to stick with something we already have, rather than pursuing something we may never get. Fear is the reason many people go through life and die full - full of ideas, dreams and talent that never got out. Why would The Mind let people die full of dreams and talents? It´s part of the puzzle - part of the cycle. All in due time and now we have dis-covered another piece and we *can* let the potential out. We *can* open the nozzle. The time is *now*.

We come here with a gift to express and experience the potential of The Mind. The No Thing wants to be Some Thing, but most people have left this Earth plane behind without manifesting the potential they came with. Was it part of The Plan too? Yes, all in due course. The characters we play in this "movie" are here for a reason. To express and do in order for The Mind to know itself and BE. The Mind experiences itself through each character in this movie and it has to forget in order to get more out of the experience. If the early humans, several thousand years ago, knew they were God in Disguise and that they could tap into this source to connect with The Mind and let all the potential out "in one go" what would have happened? Would God through us gain more or less in terms of defining Himself than with "the current model"?

What we call history and evolution would not be part of the "movie" - the cycle. The movie (cycle) would in a way "end to soon". We would re-member "too soon". One step at a time. The puzzle is being completed piece by piece. The "current model" has led us to this time of awakening, but still many let fear get the better of them. Those already awake must re-mind others that there is nothing to fear. Fear is **F**eeling **E**xcited **A**nd **R**eady as Neal Donald Walsch puts it. When you feel the fear you are challenging your ego and your status quo mindset. You are moving out of the comfort zone and into a zone of excitement. You are on the right track to create and express something new. Keep going. Don´t let the fear shut you down - don´t let the fear close the nozzle. Don´t let the fear let you die full. Way too many people die full because they give into fear. They allow fear and negative thought patterns stop them. People are afraid to think outside the box and break out of the "normal existence."

The enemy is fear. We think it is hate; but it is fear.
- Mahatma Gandhi

The fear is strong in some and less in others. For those who still feel the fear it will dictate the vibrational set-up. Vibration is the signal you send out into the Universe - to The Cosmic Mind and through the Law of Vibration and Attraction you get back what you sent out. The characters still feeling fear will need to play it out. It´s part of the set-up carried out by The Mind, but the time has come for more people to let go. As such more characters will experience the letting go of fear.

Some scientists talk of The Mind as The Unified Field. An intelligent field which we communicate with through our vibration. Whatever we are vibrating out the Field will try to provide us with. We are conscious beings and as brain scientist Candace Pert PhD says in the movie *What the Bleep Do We*

Know?

Consciousness creates reality. Consciousness is real. Consciousness obeys the laws of physics.[8]
- Candace Pert

Yes, consciousness obeys the laws of physics since consciousness requires the construct of time and space something which will be explained in detail in chapter nine *The Paradox of Creation*. The Mind sets it up for us to play the vibrational game. So the big question is: what are we vibrating out? What are we thinking and feeling at any given moment? Whatever we give energy to will manifest. This was the message from the book and movie *The Secret*. The Law of Attraction is resting on the Law of Vibration so David Icke is right:

The Prime state of everything is vibrational so that is where the game is played.
- David Icke

What we vibrate out is what we attract into our lives. If you want to change your life in this 3D experience start vibrating out whatever it is you want to experience in your life and *act* as if it has already happened. Start seeing yourselves as the one you want to be. You have an incredible power - imagination. *You have the ability to think regardless of circumstances.* You can see yourself in your mind's eye as whatever you want. It´s all about creating the feeling you will feel when you have reached your goal. The more you do this the sooner it will manifest. You hold the key. You are created in the image of God and have the powers to create, but you have to impress your thoughts and feelings upon formless substance and it will cause the thing you think and feel about to be created.

Just as Wallace D. Wattles discovered, "our thoughts and feelings are our tools to navigate the body into different experiences." This is God wanting to express Himself through you since you are God in Disguise, but you will not think in this manner if the character you play was not meant to think this way. Since you are reading this book you are meant to wake up and realize that you truly are God in Disguise. All is Mind in this creation game. The body is our vehicle. This body, with its thoughts and feelings, is just like a sailing boat with a sail and a steering wheel. If you want to sail to a specific destination you need to set the course and you need wind to get there.

Body = the sailboat
Thoughts = the mast, the sail and the steering wheel
Feelings = the wind

If you want to reach a certain goal in your life you have to set the goal - think about it and visualize it. Just like setting the course for a destination with the sailing boat. It needs a steering wheel, a mast and a sail in order to be able to go somewhere. You must think about the goal, but you will not reach your goal without feelings. Feelings = wind. Without wind you don´t go anywhere. You can steer as much as you like, but without wind you don´t move forward. This is why it ´s important to be passionate about what you want - about your goal.

The heart generates the strongest electromagnetic field in the body and sends out a strong signal to the ether - to the Universe - to The Mind about what you want. Being passionate and really doing things with your heart is what generates the wind. The more passionate you are about what you want the more wind you produce for your sailing boat. As a result you will move forward with ease and reach your destination fast. Being passionate is setting up your home frequency belonging to your soul rather than that of your mind which is your personal frequency. When creating from the heart you are in line with what God wants. You create from the uniqueness that you are and you are true to yourself. You are not copying anyone else. You are bringing some new experience to the table - something entirely new. By doing this you are completing your mission and helping The Mind to know itself - being by doing. This is the purpose of being here just like Thomas Troward wrote in *The Dore Lectures* in 1909:

The Divine operation is always for expansion and fuller expression, and this means the production of something beyond what has gone before, something entirely new, not included in past experience, though proceeding out of it by orderly sequence of growth. [24]

On your way to your destination you must *enjoy* every moment of your journey. You are here to create yourself anew and enjoy the manifestation process. Be in the now. Now is all you´ve got.

THE GIFT OF NOW

Once you have set yourself a goal and involved yourself with your feelings and your heart - just relax - let go and let God show you the magic through you. Let go of the fear. You will succeed because you have wind in your sails. Be patient. If you start doubting you are giving into fear and you stop the wind. As long as you follow your heart - your intuition - you are truly a conscious co-creator. We have reached a point in the puzzle where we start to see the bigger picture. We are getting in touch with the essence of who we are, soul, and it is seeking to be in pureness. It wants to express itself - to reveal itself - to show you that you are part of God - that you are God in Disguise and that any idea or dream that you resonate with can be brought out into this space-time construct. It can be manifested and experienced as real. Your intuition is the key.

As Penney Peirce say in her book *Frequency*:

Intuition is direct, unbiased perception that comes from unifying the fragmented parts of your awareness - body, emotions, mind and spirit - and it arises when you are focused in the present moment. [22]

Intuition is assisting you in your mission on Earth. It´s telling you what to do. It knows the part you are playing - what you came here to do. In 2004 Rita Eide published a channeled book titled *Celestial Voice of Diana*. She claims Princess Diana came to her and spoke through her. The messages were recorded and then published. One of the messages concerned intuition:

The understanding will come now where you realize that you can access your subconscious mind through your intuition and this will open up hidden parts of your own experience and everything you have suppressed. In the end this will lead you to manifest what you really want in life. [48]

The intuition knows the uniqueness you bring to life. We are all unique in the way we think and feel. Thoughts and feelings are specific electromagnetic units setting up your unique vibration. A prayer is our way to reach out and talk to God, but how can the God within talk back? God - The Mind - talks back through your intuition and this is why we are always reminded to be present - to be in the now. *Present* is a gift - the gift of God talking back through your intuition. By being here and now and in the present you are opening the communication channel to the God within you. To the

Universal Mind. You are being given a present - the ability to connect with The Mind -The Source - the No Thing that only wants to be Some Thing through you. This potential - this No Thing - is everywhere. It is always there for you.

There is never nothing going on.
-The Peaceful Warrior

In the movie *The Peaceful Warrior,* based on a true story about Dan Millman, Nick Nolte plays a mentor and humble expert on the secret of life. The message of the film is about being in the present moment, rather than living life in the past or in the future. It´s about noticing the teeming life that exists in our natural environment, about seeing the twinkle in the eyes of someone passing by, about hearing the wind talk and feeling the caress of the sun's warmth.

The teeming life, which is the Source, is constantly expressing itself through every single atom in the cosmos. In the film, Nolte makes a great comment when he sees how busy Dan Millman is, running into the future, never stopping for a moment to notice the fantastic life happening all around him. Nolte says: *There is never nothing going on.* There is something going on all the time. It is life, displaying itself in all its splendor. Life is a force constantly seeking an outlet to live more, be more and experience more, and we are the participating instruments being used for this purpose. This is why anything and everything is possible.

We just have to notice it and this requires being present. Most people are not. They are too busy thinking about the past or the future like Dan Millman was in the movie. Why is that? Why are we not present? Why are we not living in the now? The Now has power as Eckart Tolle talks about in his books. One big reason is that the society we live in stimulates our left brain much more than it does the right brain. The left brain is all about the past and the future. From birth the external world is bombarding our five senses with impressions all the time and we are told that what we see is real. Society through the educational system and through the media keeps stimulating our left brain with impressions as we grow up. Author and speaker David Icke refers to this set-up as being left brain prisoners.

The left brain is the 'rational' intellect which only believes what it can see, touch, taste, hear or smell. The education system and the media are structured for this and most teachers, lecturers, scientists and journalists are left brain prisoners themselves - David Icke [49]

Icke talks about the Elite (people with power) who runs this world because they control the masses by stimulating the left brain. If the left brain is being highly stimulated no wonder we are thinking about our past and future and forgetting the now. Without the NOW - we lose our power. We leave little room for our right brain which is all about the present moment. One who can verify this is brain researcher Dr. Jill Bolte Taylor. She is well aware of the different functions of the right and left hemisphere of our brain from a scientific point of view, but she also has "hands on" experience in how our two hemispheres of the brain work and function.

In 1996 she experienced a stroke affecting certain areas of the left side of her brain. As a brain researcher she understood what was happening, and was subsequently able to describe what she experienced when these areas in her brain became disabled. The left side of the brain is the logical, analytical and rational side. Skills such as language, science and mathematics are typical functions of the left side of the brain, while creative, musical and holistic skills are typical of the right side. Dr. Taylor explains this as follows:

Our left hemisphere thinks linearly and methodically. It's all about the past and about the future. It's designed to take that collage of the present moment, and pick out details after details, categorize them, associate them with all of what we have learned in the past, and project into our future possibilities. It thinks in languages. It's the internal chatter that connects us to the external world. It's the calculating intelligence that reminds me when I have to do my laundry. And most important it's the voice that tells me 'I am.' It is what makes us individually separate from everything around us in our world.

The right part of our brain is a totally different story, she says:

Our right hemisphere is all about this present moment. It's all about right here right now. Our right hemisphere, it thinks in pictures and it learns kinesthetically through the movement of our bodies. Information in the form of energy streams in simultaneously through all of our sensory systems. And then it explodes into this enormous collage of what this present moment looks like. What this present moment smells like and tastes like, what it feels like and what it sounds like. [50]

The right hemisphere of our brain is all about the NOW - it gives us power because we connect with The Source - with The Cosmic Mind. As Icke says:

When we open our hearts and minds we activate the right brain, the intuition and inspiration that connects with the cosmos.

The right brain is about The Now - the static now - which is the *is-ness* - the no-space/time feeling and this is freedom. No constraints, but when we are in the left brain we are in the future and in the past in our thinking and hence we are like a person in a carriage on rails. We are in bondage. No real freedom. The freedom is in the Now, but the concept of time eludes and deceives us into living for the future or thinking about the past and as such it tricks us into not living in the now. When we are in the now - in the present moment and come from the heart we open up for our intuition and the right brain which connects with The Cosmic Mind. However, if we are living most of our lives from the left brain it will trap us into the past and future. It will make us forget about the present moment - *now*. Now is a present - being present is the key. This is also why so many indigenous people around the world talk about going within. Go within and connect with your heart - with your intuition and see that you are God in Disguise.

The Great spiritual geniuses, whether it was Moses, Buddha, Plato, Socrates, Jesus, or Emerson… have taught man to look within himself to find God.
- Ernest Holmes

Indigenous people are much more in line with the cosmic powers - The Mind - with God - with the Now - than the modern, western man with all his gadgets and techno devices. We have forgotten who we are, but now we are starting to re-member. As the Hopi Indians say:

We are the ones we are waiting for.

The time to wake up and realize that we are God in Disguise is now. We are The Mind - playing out this game and the sooner we wake up the sooner the pain will go away - the suffering - because we realize that we are All One. We are like cells in a body. The goal is to equally balance our right and left brain because then we would be in our own power. We would be living out the potential of the No Thing and manifest it into Some Thing without having to hurt or manipulate or cause suffering and pain onto others. The pain can end now.

We don´t have to experience the opposites anymore. We have the memories of it. The Mind has experienced the fall in consciousness and can move on. We have lived many lives in this 3D world and can move on to another "compartment" or level of The Mind. We are actually moving along a cycle, but it seems linear. We have the future ahead of use and the past behind us so it looks linear. We are tied to time to give us this linear experience, so time must move to make us feel as if we too are moving. By being in this very linear construct we feel very linear. It´s part of the set-up. To explain more we must take a look at time.

CHAPTER EIGHT

TIME

Our world is one of space and time. Space has three dimensions: height, length and width. With his theory of relativity Einstein introduced a fourth dimension - time or space-time since space and time are linked together. Many spiritual teachers say that we are now on the threshold of moving from a third dimension to a fifth dimension. The fourth dimension, time, also goes by the name of The Rainbow Bridge because it takes us from this 3D world to a fifth dimensional world.

In a fifth dimensional world the energy is not as 'heavy' as it is in the 3D world. In the fifth dimension we exist more as lighter beings - beings of light. On the other hand, some people say that we cannot talk about a fifth dimension because there is no such thing. When we go beyond the four dimensions of height, length, width and time we eliminate linearity and counting is linearity. We cannot go from 4 to 5. There is not a fifth dimension as such since we go into a quantum state where all dimensions are interlinked. In her book *Transition Now: Redefining Duality, 2012 and Beyond* Martine Vallee refer to how the energy entity Kryon explains these dimensions and how they are all connected. Kryon is channeled by Lee Carroll and he says:

…there is no such thing as the fifth dimension. Your reality is four dimensions: height, depth, width and time. When you move to the next level of dimensionality, you eliminate linear things entirely, becoming quantum. So the next level is no longer something you can work with the way you are used to. It's not four going to five. In three-dimensional

thinking you move to the next level, but in quantum thinking there is no next level - for levels, layers and steps do not exist. Numbering and counting does not exist either, because they are linear! Therefore you cannot count to five in the next level. [52]

I our 3D world we relate to height, length, width and time. Some argue, however, that time is an illusion. In his book *The End of Time* British physicist Julian Barbour explains how time is an illusion. Many mediums channeling information from different energy entities say the same thing. It´s an illusion, but in our space-time construct time is being used to explain movement. We live in a Universe of motion. Time is actually a stream of nows. A movie is made up of frames and when they are put together it will be motion (motion pictures), but we only see one frame at a time. We are like the static lens of a camera viewing movie frames.

Life is a cycle - a circuit, but we perceive it as linear. Why? Because the cycle is very big so any part of the cycle will be perceived as linear. You seem to be in life with a future ahead and then a disappearing past due to fading memory. So you are always on the line, in the middle somehow, going somewhere, moving forwards in time. We live in a space-time construct for consciousness to experience itself. Within this space-time construct time seems linear, but when you move closer to the truth you see the complete cycle acutely. Indeed linear time reveals itself to be a construct as it loops back on itself and in that feels more like a completed written book than a linear journey page by page. Eventually we will end up where we started - when the last piece of the puzzle goes in. The Mind reboots - it starts over - another round on the cycle. The linear loops back and The Mind follows the linear so The Mind loops back with it. Consciousness has experienced itself in what seems a linear format, but it is actually a circle. And then it "bites itself in the tail" so to speak. Our past becomes our future.

When we end up at the beginning everything unravels. Why? When you see that the reality was a circuit, then of course you were created and defined only by it. Outside of the circuit you are nothing, No Thing - the un-manifested, but then as the whole condenses further you see that you actually created the circuit. You see this when you connect with God, so you made yourself up and then you lose the last of your stability. You are experiencing the end of the linear view and this is where you reach *The Paradox Point*.

The short circuit is actually a perspective, seeing the All from a linear viewpoint and it has to be linear in order to see and re-cognize, so that evokes the paradox. The linear loops back. The circuit that should be so large it seems to be a line, loops back in The Mind and joins itself, Bang! Short circuit. Paradox! Adam bites the apple. Consciousness falls - the puzzle is being smashed in order to start over again. Rebooting of the Mind. The Mind 'sleeps'- forgets.

Will every soul - every point of consciousness experience this Paradox Point? Maybe we all do, but few will come back into 'the game' to tell others about it like Steve has done. As such there is no need for each soul to either experience it or remember it. Nevertheless, some souls need to see and experience The Paradox of Creation and share it or the logic circuit never resolves and nothing will ever make sense. Steve Berg has been as close to the core (The Paradox Point) as possible. He was drawn into my life to give me insight about this experience in order for me to include it in this book and share it with others.

This book is one of many tools used by The Mind to help us move along the cycle to re-member. The content of this book will as such resonate with people who are waking up, but others hearing about the paradox might very well call this nonsense, pure fantasy and dismiss it. Those awake will probably see these people as sound asleep - lost in their own truth and in their logical thinking. However, there is no need for judgment. We all have our own perception of reality - a reality made up of a space-time construct where logic is the tool, but we are more than logic.

We are also magic and you can´t use logic to explain magic. You can use logic in order to reveal magic, but magic itself has no explanation by definition and no one will explain the mystery of the infinite not even God, God is a mystery unto itself, 'I am that I am.' Logic can´t explain anything beyond the space-time construct (the finite world) and the infinite is beyond this construct. Logic is the tool for the space-time construct and within this construct time seems to be linear, but it´s not. The infinite is like a movie that is complete, an is-ness, but then you can't know the movie that way. You have to watch it frame by frame. Pass the frames across the lens in sequence and it seems to be moving.

The infinite does not move, it 'is.' There is no void of unknown future to move into - to allow for movement, no next moment, there is no other than the infinite. The infinite is not divided into dark and light, apparent and void, all is ONE and so it is still and unobserved. The infinite 'is' and it is on one static 'now.' That's why you can't be aware of it, because awareness is a feedback loop, re-cognition, and that requires time, past present and future for the feedback! Again it's why you sleep and wake, your mind as a fractal copy of the ALL paradoxically reverberates from each contradicting state, chicken, egg, chicken, egg. The paradox never resolves. So you are awake/aware, with a sense of space-time in mind, and then you sleep with no re-cognition facility. The Sleep peels as you wake.

The infinite explodes to create a void to move into. This is the Big Bang. It´s like the Mind is asleep (infinite) and at the same time is awake (through the Big Bang - finite) - and that is the paradox. The infinite Mind becomes finite. A sleeping Mind that is also awake. The Mind needs The Paradox. If The Paradox did not see The Mind explode, if The Paradox did not have the power to destroy the Waking Mind, then nothing and no one would/could ever sleep/forget. Which is not possible. Why? Because the linear would have no tangible beginning, where did it come from?

The question (quest-I-on) only makes sense when you realize that space-time, the finite linear, begins and ends and it is "forced" into being via the conscious element of The All. It 'emerges' like a bubble from the ever constant unobservable infinite. That is its origin!

Of course the finite world has always existed since it represents The Waked Mind that can never stop moving - never go into an off mode. Since creation is a never ending cycle (circuit) The Mind has experienced endless Bing Bang events. The infinite does not have an origin; the word origin is a space-time concept. Origin asks *how long, when* - and these are elements of time, but there is no time from the infinite perspective. Time is part of the finite world - the linear view.

Hence time is a necessary part of the set-up in order for The Mind to live out its potential in this space-time construct. Time exists as a means of conveying the creative process of consciousness. Consciousness facilitates itself by having this space-time construct in place as a playground - a doing environment. It all boils down to being by doing.

TIME AS A RIVER

In our experience we need time to create, to do and to experience in order to be. Without time there is no awareness - no feedback loop. *Time = Tie me*. I will elaborate on this in chapter nine. We are tied to time to give us the linear experience. Time must move to make us feel as if we too are moving, and via the construct time seems to move in a very constant way. If time is like water it could flow like a river and we are carried along with it. In the river you feel the current.

Current also meaning *belonging to the present time.* You are feeling the now (current) by experiencing day after day because you are being carried along by time, the current. It is moving you along. You move with the river - with the current - with time.

In our world we have three dimensions - length, depth (height) and width. The fourth dimension is time. In our river analogy the river itself is the three dimensions with length, depth and width and the current is time dragging you along - the fourth dimension. What happens when the river reaches the sea? What is the sea? What is beyond the four dimensions? A linear view would be entering into the fifth dimension, but the 3D river floats into the sea of many dimensions - a 'multidimensional sea.' In the sea there is no current. At least you don't feel it as you did in the 3D river. So how do you experience time when the water (time) does not move as it did in 3D? The answer is that you move about *in it.* Therefore, we can see our space-time bubble, our universe as an endless circular river and it never stops moving, and yet in truth it is only water. This is the linear view with past, present and future. We are in a river floating along, but in the end it loops back on itself.

People with near-death experiences say they have been out of time. There was no time and they felt one with everything. Where did they 'go?' When they died where did they end up? They ended up in the metaphoric sea. They were floating around in the 3D river (Earth) and "experiencing" the river - but when dying they moved out of the current and into the sea. In the river we are always seemingly going somewhere, which is tied to our belief in reality which itself is the river (of time). Whereas in the sea, we can swim about and never really go anywhere, especially if we see the sea as endless, where could we be going, ultimately?

When you move out of the 3D river the feeling of being dragged along by the current stops and this is the same as feeling time stopping since current = time. The river ends up in the sea - calmness. Melted in - no current, but the water is still there, it's just not "moving" as it was in the 3D river. It´s an experience being outside the river. This is exactly what has been channeled through the medium Jill Mara from *Simion, The 7th Dimensional Light Beings* in her book *Keys to Soul Evolution*:

When you step out of existing constructs, the past, present, and future are as fluid as the ocean. [30]
- Simion, The 7th Dimensional Light Beings.

When people with near-death experiences have been in this 'sea' it´s like no time exists. This sea is so big that they see no reflected movement. The only movement they see is their own 'splashing.' They move about in the sea. In other words they move about in time. The sea or the water is symbolic for The One to swim in the sea to see and love itself through the different points of consciousness - soul aspects. There is no water in the core, and where there is no water there is no life. Water is space-time (or time-space) and souls are the copies of The One Mind moving about (fragmentation).

THE FIFTH DIMENSION

In our 3D world we need time to create and experience our creation. We have the opportunity to observe ourselves progressing in a linear way. In our 3D world we can see how consciousness affects our reality. What we think and feel has an impact on our reality.

Physicality is a stage for the play of creation and you have the ability to express yourself within it. [30]
- Simion, The 7th Dimensional Light Beings.

This is the purpose - to create, to do, to experience in order to BE and we have done this for a long time in this 3D reality. We have had a long interaction with the polarized third dimensional reality with many incarnations of being either male or female. As we now move along the cycle and progress toward our return to the fifth dimension or next level we begin to lose our need and desire for a polarized expression. We will blend more into Oneness since we will understand that we are all points of consciousness in The One Mind. There is a Shift in Consciousness going on and we are "moving into the fifth dimension", but what is this fifth dimension? A dimension is a measurable component of 'reality' within this space-time construct. We tend to think of the fifth dimension as higher on the scale than the third dimension, but is it? All dimensions exist at the same time - they are entangled, but then again dimensions don´t really exist because All is Mind. It´s a way to explain the different areas or compartments of The Mind we experience. What is beyond the fourth dimension? Is there a fifth dimension? What would that be?

All is Mind, so in a so-called fifth dimension we would be experiencing another part of The Mind. We would perceive ourselves to be lighter than we are in the third dimension and "more connected" to The Mind. Spiritual teachers say we are made of light, but we are really made of Mind, as Steve experienced. I want to share his views on this:

'Light is mind; you are your own light source, think about it. If you close your eyes and imagine an image, what is illuminating that image, you can't see a light source can you, because you are the light source, you are the illumination of your own mind. All that exists is light, endless unstoppable light. Well yes, if mind is light then it makes sense. Darkness is a lie, it's achieved via exploding the mind, severing the connections in order to forget, so metaphorically it's darkness, but the darkness never holds, because the truth is light, the light we snap back when the mechanism of our hiding from the truth in order to be fails.

The light is truth, we are the truth, we are all that is and we are eternal. It's not equal, the default is light and it never, ever, ever goes out, you can never ever turn it off, existence I mean. Therefore it's we who have to hide from it, maybe looking like the metaphoric ostriches with their heads buried in the sand. Symbolic of all those who think that God can't see them as they can't see God. A funny view is that we think that God the constant goes away…Whereas God may well ask us, "*Where do you keep going to?*" because God is always there, a constant. It's us who leave and return. And yes, we perceive ourselves to have light bodies, but what are these bodies made of? They are not solid; they are made of energy oscillating, which is Mind. Our light bodies are no more real than our fleshy ones, how could they be? They are just symbols, a format for communication past the dense manifest. And that we won't look like weird 'floaty' beings when we shift.

We will look much the same as we do now. Seeing as we went to all that trouble to ground and accept the format. But then you won't be alive, and you won't be dead. You can't get killed when you are past life, which also speaks volumes as the wonders of this construct we are in now, how so? Well, take motorcycle racing for instance. If you couldn't die or get hurt, everyone would be going flat out, no fear you see. But then if you were world champion in this place, then that was a 'real' achievement. If you come off the bike at 200mph, you will be in bad shape. I doubt we will use much of the magic in the next realms, why? Because it's cheating, and it renders everything pointless.

What if football had no rules, would it be worth playing, the rules make for the game? I suggest that out and out magic is reserved for the last stages before the fall, indeed the magic contributes to the fall why? Because magic is the most addictive drug ever! You can do whatever you like. Whatever you like. Manifest your wildest fantasies, so you can see how it leads to emptiness, pointlessness. Much like how some rich and famous people can lose the plot and turn to drugs etc., in order to try to fill the void in their lives. And when I say that we won't use much magic, I mean that we won't be allowed to use it as God is Our commander still. God will protect us from that trap, we won't go from a lump of flesh to Merlin the Magician in one step.

This shift is going to be somewhat scary. Like the first day at school, but then scary good! God will slow us up after all, where's the rush past life? We will have all the time we can handle! And less really is more; we will be able to re-lax. So, a light body as in that you know it's not real is all, and you can't kill it physically, it's just a projection of The Mind. The Mind is the more real part, and even that is a construct. Indeed everything we are speaking about amounts to more symbolic ways to understand and communicate, none of it is real other than consciousness. It's all just ways to glimpse the infinite.»

We float with the river of time and as our consciousness rises we experience other realties - what many call dimensions. At present humans constitute a limited form of intelligence operating within a narrow spectrum of consciousness. We operate in the third dimension of consciousness and we exist here to create, to do and to experience. God, The One Mind, is always for creating and experience and is doing it through every point of consciousness within the different spectrums of consciousness.

Our 3D world is very dense and 'slow' and in that it takes a lot of time to manifest an idea. When you get a great idea - when it appears in your mind - you probably want to manifest it and realize it as soon as possible. However this process from idea to manifestation takes a long time. It´s a slow process since we live in a very dense reality. When we acquire higher consciousness - when we have a higher frequency - the

159

manifestation process speeds up since the "doing environment" (dimension) we experience is not as slow and dense as the 3D world.

We are moving along on a spiral back to the starting point. As we solve the puzzle piece by piece and start to re-member more and more everything speeds up. It becomes easier and easier to find the last missing pieces in the puzzle and put them in. The so-called fifth dimension is less dense than the third dimension. As such we can manifest faster. To perceive and 'be' in the fifth dimension requires a high frequency. Lower frequencies associated with fear (worry, guilt, shame, anger etc.) will not be able to exist here. As such we will be creating from our heart (no fear) for the benefit of all. We will be creating Heaven on Earth in this dimension.

The fifth dimension is just another spectrum of consciousness - another "compartment" of The Mind. The Mind has many areas to explore - many dimensions. They are like interactive programs. It might be perceived as places that generate the interaction so we can create and experience in these different densities or dimensions. We are points of consciousness having a space-time experience on this huge circle which we perceive as linear. Within The Mind these compartments interlink in order to facilitate more life because life is bigger than just this 3D world. There is a system over and above the manifested 3D world. It's like Jesus said:

In my Father's house are many rooms; if it were not so, I would have told you. I am going there to prepare a place for you. [51]

Where did Jesus go to prepare for us? He went to another compartment of The Mind - what many would call a higher dimension. Did he then go to the so-called fifth dimension or a higher one, or maybe several since they are interlinked?

Kryon addresses the nature of dimensions and how they are all interlinked. In her book *Transition Now: Redefining*

Duality, 2012 and Beyond Martine Vallée has included information from Kryon channeled through Lee Carroll where he talks about the so-called fifth dimension. Kryon says:

..there is no such thing as the fifth dimension. Your reality is four dimensions: height, depth, width and time. When you move to the next level of dimensionality, you eliminate linear things entirely, becoming quantum. So the next level is no longer something you can work with the way you are used to. It´s not four going to five. In three-dimensional thinking you move to the next level, but in quantum thinking there is no next level - for levels, layers and steps do not exist. Numbering and counting does not exist either, because they are linear! Therefore you cannot count to five in the next level. [52]

According to Kryon there is actually no fifth dimension. When we go beyond 4D, we eliminate linearity, and counting is a linearity. Counting works in our 3D world, but after the fourth dimension we go quantum. 1,2,3,4 .... Quantum. We go into multidimensionality. It's not just a "next step," either. It's the step that differentiates you from one who is in duality (our world), and one who is not. In our previous PC-Word analogy it would be the original word document (our 3D duality world) differentiated from all the other copies (multi-dimensional).

All the so-called dimensions are interwoven - they criss-cross each other like in a hank of wool. Layer upon layer, crossing over and under - no linear fashion what so-ever. As human beings we tend to look at dimension as one on top of another. We think in a linear fashion, but once past the fourth dimension it becomes multidimensional. The linear thinking is not suitable beyond this point. As such dimensions are more fluid-like and only separated by frequency. In our 3D river example it would be the same as moving into the sea. When you move into the sea you will feel lighter and you will not see it as moving. The strong current is gone. You are not being dragged along as in the 3D river, but you move about in the sea. Instead of being moved along *by time* you move about *in time*. However, time can´t cease to exist. Why? Because consciousness needs movement - it needs time to be reflected. This will be described in detail in chapter nine. As long as consciousness is self-aware time is present. As long as a soul is aware in the multidimensional sea then time and movement exist. It´s part of the construct.

When you leave the 3D river you move around in a certain part of the sea. Where in the sea you end up is determined by your frequency. The so-called dimensions are separated by frequency -vibrational speed. They have their own frequency. You will end up in a part of the sea that matches your frequency. Several spiritual teachers talk about how we must raise our frequency if we are to move into a higher dimension. They say that these dimensions are separated by zones or voids. Drunvalo Melchizedek is such a spiritual teacher. He is the author of the books *The Ancient Secrets of the Flower of Life* and he talks about how there is a zone or void between the different dimensions. The dimensions move on one level according to the chromatic scale. He speaks of The Void that separates The Whole Note Universes.

These Whole Note Universes are akin to an Octave in The Musical Scale. There is a Void between each Dimensional Level ....each time one passes from one Dimension or Overtone into the next, you must traverse this Void......All these Dimensions inter-penetrate each other, such that they all exist at every point in space. One need not go anywhere to gain access to these other Dimensions because they are accessible to you from within. [53]

Yes, we can access these from within since all is Mind. It´s like The Mind has compartments and in order to experience a certain compartment you must change your level of vibration. You must pass through "the zone/void" as Drunvalo talks about. You must raise and expand your consciousness and what you perceive as your reality will change. You will then be granted access to another part of The Mind.

The sea is connected to everything - to the 3D river floating into the sea and to everything else (the other dimensions). As such you will be multi-dimensional once you are in this sea, but the part of the sea you are moving about in will determine what you have conscious access to. As such beings in the 3D river would not have access to the sea unless they raise their frequency. Beings in what people call fifth dimension would not have access to another part of the sea called the sixth dimension and so on. As such the sea works as a model to explain the dimensions because the dimensions are all connected to each other. They are fluid like, interwoven and hence we can't use a linear explanation. However they are separated by frequency - different parts of the sea - all interlinked - all is water. Or like the hank of wool - layer upon layer, crossing over and under - no linear fashion. All intertwined.

The sea is an ever expanding understanding and mixture of consciousness. Once in the sea you are conscious of your own movements or splashes in this area of the sea. Being in the sea - being fluid and connected to everything would be what Quantum Physics call a wave. This field of science has shown how a particle can be both a particle and a wave. Could it be that our 3D river is the particle world and the sea is the wave world? Yes, if we look at it as Space-Time *vs.* Time-Space as the American engineer Dewey B. Larson did. We observe space as being three-dimensional, but space does not exist without time, therefore time must be three-dimensional as well, Larson dis-covered.

SPACE-TIME and TIME-SPACE

The physical reality has three dimensions of space: length, width and height (depth), plus one dimension of time. Albert Einstein introduced the fourth dimension in physics—what he called space-time. In 1905 he published his Theory of Relativity in which he linked space and time. He said that space and time were not actually separate and he placed them together in one dynamic unit. Einstein regarded this as a fabric woven together from space and time to form a sort of "carpet." He then introduced gravitation and its effect on this space-time carpet. According to Einstein the planets in the universe are sunk into this space-time carpet—they do not just float around in empty space in the universe. This space-time carpet is curved in the presence of matter. It can respond dynamically by either contracting or expanding.

Here on Earth we can move around in a three-dimensional world, and the Earth moves around our solar system in the same three-dimensional world. In this space-time reality, time is one-dimensional and is locked. *Time = Tie - Me*. It ties you up. You cannot move around in time. You cannot go to the past or the future - you are "dragged along" by the current (time) in the 3D river. In his book *The Source Field investigations* author and speaker David Wilcock explains that the opposite of space-time is time-space. He refers to Dewey B. Larson's work on this subject: The Reciprocal System of Theory. Dewey B. Larson (1898-1990) was an American engineer and the originator of The Reciprocal System of Theory, a comprehensive theoretical framework capable of explaining all physical phenomena from subatomic particles to galactic clusters.

In this general physical theory space and time are simply the two reciprocal aspects of the sole constituent of the universe: motion. [54]
- *Dewey B. Larson.*

The thesis of The Reciprocal System is that the Universe is not a Universe of matter, but a Universe of motion, one in which the basic reality is motion, and all entities—photons, particles, atoms, fields, forces, and all forms of energy— are merely manifestations of motion. Space and time are the two reciprocal aspects of this motion, and cannot exist independently. As you will see in chapter nine *The Paradox of Creation* consciousness requires time, which is movement, to exist - to be aware of itself - a recognized though - a feedback loop. As such Larson´s theory saying that the sole constituent of the Universe is motion makes sense.

We observe space as being three-dimensional, but space does not exist without time, therefore time must be three-dimensional as well. This discovery opened the door to the world of quantum physics, where experiments showed that particles such as electronics (electrons = matter) behaved like waves. They appeared to float around instead of behaving like fixed matter, shifting between these two states. These discoveries of the behavior of subatomic particles are the results of scientists digging deeper into the nature of energy patterns and they are able to perceive time-space energy patterns in physical manifestation in space.

Time-space is the inverse of space-time. In our daily lives we move in space, while time is constant. One might say that space-time is the reality we live in now - our everyday waking reality of planet earth. We move about in space. Here - on earth - in space-time, we have control over space, in that we can move our bodies freely from one place to another. However, we cannot move about in time. We experience time as a linear phenomenon and we have no control over it. When the term *time-space* is used, it refers to the metaphysical universe - 'the other side'.

In this 'reality' space is fixed and we can move about in time, just like moving around in the multidimensional sea.

This is what we experience when we dream. We can suddenly be in what we regard as being the past and then all of a sudden we find ourselves in another time zone. Everything is happening now. Time is not linear. Here on Earth time appears to be linear because we are in the space-time reality, but in the time-space reality time is not linear. Everything actually happens now—the past, present and future are connected.

In this time-space reality, it´s possible to see forwards and backwards in time. In this state we are in the sea and everything is connected - the water - time - is everywhere and we are in it - splashing and moving about in time. People with NDE experience of 'the other side' say they went through a life review where they saw all their lives. They had the experience of all lifetimes as if all of them were occurring at the same time.

According to Larson someone being in time-space would appear to us on Earth as being a wave. A wave is like fluid - connected to everything. A particle is not. It is solid and separated from its surroundings - or at least it seems so. Someone being in this time-space reality would as such be connected to everything and would have the feeling that time did not exist as we know it - just like in the analogy of the sea. The current stops. They would be able to move around in what we call past, present and future.

Anyone who tunes into this time-space reality will therefore be able to obtain information about what, in our reality, we call the future. Prophets, fortune tellers, clairvoyants, the Mayans and other indigenous peoples have been able to tune into the time-space reality by meditating or taking substances that stimulate the pineal gland. They have thus been able to provide us with an insight into what could happen in the future - the next step on the cycle.

The separation between time-space and space-time is not a clear-cut distinction. No either or - no fixed dividing line.

Time-space is that which surrounds us. It permeates all of space-time and we wouldn't be able to be in space-time without also being part of time-space - we enter this realm every night. I know many people with extraordinary psychic abilities, including my wife, who are able to tap into the time-space realm and communicate with beings 'there.' And likewise there are beings in time-space that can connect with us in this space-time reality.

In the midst of all this we must not forget that All is Mind and that space-time and time-space realities are nothing but illusions. When I say that space-time is within time-space I am actually saying that it is an illusion within an illusion. Everything we experience either in space-time or time-space is not real. It is a construct for The One Mind to experience itself. More about that in the next chapter. However, as human beings we need a format so we can understand more of creation and all these realities - hence the space-time vs. time-space explanation.

People with near-death experiences say they became one with everything and everyone when being on 'the other side.' They say they *were consciousness*. They were thoughts. Could it be that we come from a time-space reality where we exist before we come to this three-dimensional world—into a space-time reality? According to author and speaker Michelle Belanger we do. Time-space describes how we experience ourselves in between lives. The process of incarnation involves a transition from time-space to space-time. I met Michelle while she did an interview on TV a few years ago. She told me she remembers all her previous lives on Earth and when we die we don't go anywhere:

You don't really go anywhere—you are in between spaces and you are one with everything.
- Michelle Belanger

This agrees with what P.M.H. Atwater discovered when she was engaged in her mammoth task involving people who have had near-death experiences. She interviewed 3,000 people with NDE and they told her they could hear all thoughts and they felt connected to everything and everyone. Yes, because we are consciousness. We are part of The Cosmic Mind. This Mind needs the space-time construct to experience itself. As such The Mind can experience itself in what we call space-time (our reality on Earth −3D river), but also in time-space (the sea). When we die the body is left behind, but the consciousness continues to experience itself in another realm - another reality. Another copy of the real 3D world. Another room in the house of The Father.

As long as consciousness is self-aware it must be in a space-time/time-space construct - in the finite world - The Waked Mind. Consciousness cannot be self-aware in the infinite world - The Sleeping Mind. People with near-death experiences say they were aware of themselves on the other side. They were conscious even though they were dead. As such they must have been in the space-time/time-space construct - in the finite world created for The Mind to experience itself. The finite world is then composed of different realities and we, as point of consciousness, experience these realities. No point of consciousness (soul) can experience complete timelessness. As long as you are aware you recognize, and recognition is a feedback mechanism (feedback loop) that requires time.

As we shall see in the next chapter time and space are quantifications which cannot exist in the infinite world. The infinite world is pure potential. It is the potential of the cosmic mind to be anything. However in order to create, to produce and do things the mind needs space and time. In other words, it requires a finite world - a creation environment where God can live out the infinite potential that God has. As a result the infinite world "forces" the production of space-time bubble which we call the Big Bang. And this is the paradox - an infinite mind which is not conscious 'creates' a finite world so it can be conscious and aware of its creation. The cycles of creation are therefore driven by the core paradox of the infinite and the finite. A cosmic mind that is both asleep and awake at the same time.

CHAPTER NINE

THE PARADOX OF CREATION

My view of creation as outlined in this chapter is a truth shared with my good friend Steve Berg from UK. Steve had an experience of expanded consciousness many years ago giving him an incredible insight to what creation is all about. I have met many people with near-death experiences, but Steve was not one of them. His experience was something else. I have yet to meet anyone with a similar mind-blowing experience. He says he came as close to the core of creation - The Paradox Point - as it is possible to get. I have spent months corresponding with Steve and enjoyed his incredible insight and wisdom. He has been able to provoke thought in me, as I have in him. Many of the paragraphs in this chapter are excerpts from our correspondence. Right now you might think that I am referring to Steve´s experience as a testimonial to the one and only truth of creation. I´m not. Steve has given me his insight and his truth and this truth resonates with me. I share his truth about the core and the paradox of creation. It is our truth, but that doesn't mean it will be accepted by everyone who reads this book. All we ask is for you to keep an open mind. See what resonates with you.

Creation: the act of producing or causing to exist;

Who or what produced the Universe? How did this Universe come into existence? By cosmic coincidence or by intelligent design? A random event or one that was planned? Where do we actually come from? What is our origin? The answer defines what it means to be a human being. Various theories exist about our origins, and obviously this affects our attitude to life. Our origins are decisive for our understanding of who we actually are and what we are doing here. Such possible origins are also the subject of considerable debate between those who look from a scientific point of view and those who adopt a religious stance.

Do we believe that our Universe has been created by pure chance and that Darwin's Theory of Evolution is correct, or do we believe that there is a creator behind everything that exists? Is life a coincidence or not? Our beliefs will determine our views about where we come from - the origin of the Universe. It is widely accepted that it all started with the Big Bang. This event is the greatest mystery of all times and the more scientists learn the deeper the mystery becomes. Current science suggests that the Big Bang explosion/expansion occurred about 13.7 billion years ago, but how do they know this? They know the Universe is expanding due to the discovery made by Edwin Hubble. During the 1920's and 30's, Edwin Hubble discovered that the Universe is expanding, with galaxies moving away from each other at a velocity given by an expression known today as Hubble's Law.

By studying the way in which the Universe expands cosmologists said it was possible to learn a great deal about its past and as such to trace the expansion back to its point of origin - the Big Bang. Much like you would be able to rewind a video showing an explosion. Cosmologists have calculated the Big Bang event to app. 13.7 billion years ago and they say they know what happened just a billionth of a second after the explosion/expansion. However, they don´t know what preceded the Big Bang. How did the Big Bang occur? What went bang? Some scientists have come up with the bouncing universe theory. What went bang is replaced with why does it bounce?

According to some oscillatory universe theorists, the Big Bang was simply the beginning of a period of expansion that followed a period of contraction. In this view, one could talk of a Big Crunch followed by a Big Bang, or more simply, a Big Bounce. This suggests that we could be living at any point in an infinite sequence of universes, or conversely the current universe could be the very first iteration. (Source: Wikipedia) [6]

But how and why did it all start? In their book *The Grand Design*, Stephen Hawking and Leonard Mlodinow, argue that the Big Bang, rather than occurring following the intervention of a divine being, was inevitable due to the law of gravity. The laws of physics can explain, they say, how a Universe of space, time and matter could emerge spontaneously, without the need for God. Most cosmologists agree. They say we don't need a god-of-the-gaps to make the Big Bang go bang. It can happen as part of a natural process. Hawking and Mlodinow argue that because there is a law like gravity, the Universe can and will create itself from nothing.

Their basic argument is that there must be a law of gravity. The law of gravity must take a particular form and because there must be such a law, the Universe created itself out of nothing. But then where did the law come from? So it's not really an origin theory is it? Furthermore, spontaneous creation is the reason there is something rather than nothing, why the universe exists, why we exist. It is not necessary to invoke God to light the blue touch paper and set the Universe going, they say. [7]
Their idea of nothing isn't really nothing. It includes at least a law of gravity. They are defining nothing so it complies with the laws of physic to dismiss a Creator - a God. They aren't really starting with nothing at all. Where did this law of gravity come from? They say that such a law must exist. How can that be? Nothing stays no-thing. It doesn´t include a

scientific law. It seems like they got blinded by their own truth - blinded by logic. If some "thing" constant exists and because nothing can come from nothing, then something must have always existed! It seems they are thinking that the law in itself is what forces the manifest in order for the law to be played out and exist. If the law exists then the Universe has to envelope it, facilitate it.

However, no thing would have to remain nothing, if the Universe could emerge spontaneously out of nothing - out of the void - out of the vacuum - where is the action? There is no action in nothing. How could the Universe explode and expand out of nothing? There is no action in nothing to then flip it over into a something. Nothing stays no-thing. When you realize that, as nothing can come out from nothing, then a nothing would have to have stayed nothing. This will bring you to the understanding that because something exists, because you exist, as you are then your own witness. Then something must have always existed! There is something in nothing! The answer comes via the understanding that what we see as nothing is actually the infinite, which can't manifest!.

In Hinduism they talk about how God - Brahman - is breathing in and out. Breathing out being symbolic of The Big Bang expansion and breathing in when everything contracts. Everything is in motion. Hinduism views the world as an ever changing and fluid manifestation of the powerful magic of Brahman. Nothing ever stands still.

Neal Donald Walsch also talks about breathing in and out of God in his book *Conversations with God:*

Neal: Is the Universe now expanding?
God: At a rate of speed you cannot imagine!
Neal: Will it expand forever?
God: No. There will come a time when the energies driving the expansion will dissipate, and the energies holding things together will take over—

pulling everything "back together" again.
Neal: You mean the Universe will contract?
God: Yes. Everything will, quite literally, "fall into place"! And you'll have paradise again. No matter. Pure energy…….

Neal: What will happen after the Universe "collapses"?
God: The whole process will start over again! There will be another so-called Big Bang, and another Universe will be born. It will expand and contract. And then it will do the same thing all over again. And again. And again. Forever and ever. World without end. This is the breathing in and breathing out of God. [4]

Are the ancient scriptures from Hinduism and other religions right when they say that God created the Universe? Or is current science correct? Did the Universe come out of nothing? *Both are correct!* Science is correct since the Universe did indeed come from nothing, it´s just that their definition of nothing is incorrect. Nothing in the case of creation is in fact the infinite state! No Thing – an unlimited potential – but not manifest.

Mind is apparent even before it defines and formulates a thought, thought is structure manifest within the abstract mind. - Steve Berg

The Universe was un-manifest prior to the Big Bang - No Thing turned into Some Thing when the Big Bang occurred. Abstract becoming concrete, and in order for this to happen there must be intelligent design behind all of creation - a creator - a God. God is realizing His potential by creating a space-time construct - a doing and creating environment in order to manifest the un-manifested.

If God did not exist it would be necessary to invent him. But all nature cries aloud that he does exist; that there is a supreme intelligence, an immense power, an admirable order, and everything teaches us our own

dependence on it. [58]
- Voltaire (François-Marie-Arouet).

NO THING

When we break down the word *nothing* we get *No Thing*. So, yes the Big Bang came out of nothing because it´s not *a thing yet*. It´s a *potential* waiting to become *Some Thing*. It´s a concept. It is not yet tangible. Not concrete. Even at the concept stage it's already defined within the mind, therefore what we see as real, as we are part of the manifest, is really just a concept. It's not physical per se. No Thing is actually *infinite potential consciousness*.

No physical thing - no experience in the physical - just a potential. You can´t touch it, feel it, see it. It´s like the mind - you can´t see the mind, but we know it´s 'there.' We have a mind, but we can´t locate it or see it. Where is it? And this is the clue to creation itself. Everything you see (and not see) is *mind*. All is Mind. This One Mind exists and for no reason with no origin. It´s like magic. We are indeed magical at base.

It´s like the Queen song: *It's a kind of magic - There can be only One.*

Even logic has to logically concede the fact that anything standing as a reason for an origin, would itself require its own origin, and therefore all you would ever see is an infinite cascade. Therefore there can be no logical origin! Ergo, logic recognizes magic which by definition has no logical cause.
- Steve Berg

Everything in our Universe is consciousness. This was presented by many different scientists in the 2004 movie *What the Bleep Do We Know!?* - a movie looking into the weird world of quantum physics saying that we are all part of universal consciousness. The inner world creates the outer world. In the movie Professor of Physics John Hagelin says:

Our Universe is like a thought wave, an invisible state or quantum wave spread over time and space. Not a wave of matter. But wave in what? In a universal ocean—an ocean of pure potentiality—a unified field—a superstring field of which we are all made. [8]

As he says: *an ocean of pure potentiality.* This potential - this No Thing wants to be Some Thing. This nothing is the glue that holds everything. It is the non-space which holds the space and it is everywhere. It's like the air. It is within us, around us and it is always seeking an outlet. It wants to get out and be experienced through you. What good is a potential if it's not realized? The very act of experiencing this potential is what life is all about. You get an idea or you have a dream.

Where did that idea or dream come from? From your subconscious mind? How did it end up there? It is God, The Cosmic Mind, seeking an outlet to experience itself. When you get an idea it is God within you wanting to experience Himself. Why? God must do this in order to feel how it is to BE!

God is All That Is, but if All That Is has not been experienced then it is just a potential - infinite - unlimited - un-manifested potential. It is a knowing without experience. Potential capable of being, but not yet manifest. Potential means having the power or being capable of happening. It's like knowing without the hands-on experience - theory and practice. You can know yourself to be kind, but unless you do something to demonstrate your kindness you have not completed the knowing. You just have a concept - an idea about what kindness is. You need the experience to *really know.*

For instance - it's possible for you to have the knowledge

on how to ride a bike, because you have read about it. You have seen others do it. You have studied it, but until you actually do it yourself you have no experience of it - theory and practice. Or you might know yourself to be a great artist - a great painter. You have the potential to paint like Michelangelo, but how do you *really know* until you actually do it - experience it? You have the knowing, but after doing it, by creating it you also gain the experience. Then it becomes complete - potential being realized.

God is the Creator and creates through you and me. God is The Mind. We are sole thoughts, we are the interaction. All is Mind. The Absolute. All That Is. The Mind of God wants to create and the act of creating involves doing it - getting the experience, and by doing it God, as the No Thing, can really know how it is to *be* Some Thing - Any Thing - Every Thing. God is getting to really know it self by doing - by creating and gaining experience. With the memory of actually creating and living out an experience from its potential it will finally BE. As Shakespeare said: To Be or Not to Be - that is the question.

The whole purpose is then to enjoy every second of the manifestation process. We are here to enjoy the slow process of creating since this involves an experience which contributes to being. This is why we need to be present in the Now. We must notice the actual process of creation as we create - how it is manifesting here in our dense, physical world. An idea becomes a reality. This is the joy - this is the ride God wants in order to complete Himself. Having unlimited - un-manifested potential in itself is not enough. It must be experienced and enjoyed leading to completeness - BEING. It boils down to *being by doing.*

In order for God to *be* God must do, create and experience. This requires a doing environment - a place to experience its potential so that No Thing can be Some Thing - Any Thing - Every Thing. God needs "a mirror" - a reflection to see Himself, but The Mind is All That Is - The Absolute -

so how can a reflection exist outside The Mind to allow for this reflection - this doing? After all, how can there be something outside All That Is?

REFERENCE POINT FROM WITHIN

A reference point from within is needed. It´s part of this set-up for God to experience itself. There must be a place (space) allowing for time to exist because in order to create - to do - to experience - we need time - a linear format - a space-time construct. Some measure of time must pass from when an idea is born in our minds to when it is let out and manifested. As such time is subject to existence, but existence is not subject to time. The time and space construct is a concept bubble within existence. Existence just IS and it has always been. It's infinite! That's why it can't manifest as the infinite can't be quantified - defined and time is a definition so no, the infinite is not, indeed cannot be subject to time! It's an *is-ness* a constant that can't be re-cognized as re-cognition requires time, and of course space, time-space. The Nothingness has always been. No start - no beginning. Creation through the space-time construct happens within this is-ness within existence. It´s even shown in the English language. Within the word **Infinite** we find the finite - the space-time construct created for The Mind to live out its infinite potential. In-finite. As such a hole in the whole is created.

We live in this space-time construct and we are all tapping into The Mind of God because we are The Mind, God in Disguise, wanting to realize its potential. In disguise in the sense that we are pretending that there is more than one of us here! We are varied aspects of the same one consciousness, varied in order to create a catalyst for exploration of what consciousness may be this via the interactive scenarios our differences create. God - the infinite, unlimited, un-manifested potential consciousness has set-up a finite world to achieve this format - this reference point. This is The Big Bang seemingly appearing out of the nothingness. God is No Thing - yet. Just a potential - a concept.

As such God must have a realm where God can be aware and conscious of Himself by doing, creating and experiencing. The No Thing can *be* Some Thing. Creation is realized and No Thing becomes Every Thing - ALL starting with a tiny speck of super-hot energy evolving into Every Thing in our great Universe. Space-time is the construct which is needed for God to realize its potential. It´s the playground for enjoying the manifestation process. God is thus All and Nothing (the manifested and the un-manifested).

The infinite has no time or space. Creating something and being aware of the creating in order to gain experience is thus not possible in the infinite. Hence, the need for the finite realm where the potential and the un-manifested can turn into something concrete and manifested in a linear format with space and time as the necessary elements.

Neal Donald Walsch has also touched upon the need for a finite realm in order for God to create. In his book *Conversation with God* he uses the terms absolute and relative to describe this. In answering Neal God is saying:

The realm of the relative was created in order that I might experience My Self…
…This does not make the realm of the relative real. It is a created reality you and I have devised and continue to devise—in order that we may know ourselves experientially. Yet the creation can seem very real. Its purpose is to seem so real, we accept it as truly existing. In this way, God has contrived to create "something else" other than Itself. In creating "something else"—namely, the realm of the relative—I have produced an environment in which you may choose to be God, rather than simply

be told that you are God…[4]

Walsch mentioned that the relative (the finite) *was* created - that God *had* produced an environment in which we may choose to be God. However, this implies time and thus a "starting point". So when did this "wanting to experience itself" occur? When was the finite, relative reality created? It can´t *have been* created since it has always been. God is The Mind - All is Mind. We can´t see or locate the starting point of creation because there is no starting point in a mind. A mind goes on forever, no boundaries. No start - no end - infinite. Time begins and ends, but 'what is' is a constant!

In our finite world cosmologists relate to the Big Bang as our starting point, but since All is Mind there is no starting point. It only looks like a starting point seen from within the space-time construct - from our 3D perspective. There are many Big Bangs and they are all part of an eternal cycle of expansion and contraction. This space-time "bubble" is expanding and contracting all the time. This is also supported by some physicist one of them being mathematical physicist Neil Turok, a teacher at Cambridge University. He says:

The Big Bang was big, but it wasn't the beginning. Our Big Bang represents just one stage in an infinitely repeated cycle of universal expansion and contraction. There have been many Big Bangs, and there will be many more. [9]

Together with another distinguished theoretical physicists, Paul J. Steinhardt (Princeton University), they published their book *Endless Universe: Beyond the Big Bang* in 2007 where they argue that there is a series of Big Bangs happening over and over again, back and forth across potentially infinite time. Right now we are inside such a 'Big Bang bubble'- our 3D reality - the current space-time construct where science has calculated "a starting point" which is The Big Bang happening app. 13.7 billion years ago. But what went bang? In order to explain we have to realize that creation itself is a paradox.

THE INFINITE AND THE FINITE

God the infinite - needs the finite, relative world to mirror Himself - to create, to experience, to do in order to be. As such the cycles of creation are driven by the core paradox of the infinite and the finite. This can be explained in five steps:

1. All is Mind. Absolutely everything.

2. This Mind is infinite and the infinite is an unknowable state. You can´t understand it - know it or quantify it. As such *time and space* cannot exist in the infinite because they are quantifications and belong to the finite world. The known world.

3. This Mind is conscious. The Mind is everything including you and you are conscious. So the Mind is conscious.

4. Consciousness requires *space and tim*e in order to be conscious. Space and time belong to the finite world since they are quantifications.

5. The paradox is a fact since there is an infinite Mind that is also conscious, but consciousness requires time and space which belong to the finite world. The Mind is both infinite and finite. And that is impossible. You can´t be your own defining opposite. Not from the same perspective. You can´t be cold *and* hot at the same time. It is a paradox.

The Mind is both infinite and finite. And it will always contain each element, this because it is conscious which requires space-time for feedback (finite) and yet you can't logically end or size (quantify) a mind (infinite). It is the Yin-Yang. But why does consciousness require space-time? Why is it tied to space-time? In order for you to be conscious of something you need space and time. Space in order to view the something to be conscious of. Consciousness is achieved via the mind having the ability to separate into viewer and view-screen aspects.

In order to have consciousness you have to have separation. You´ve got to have more than one thing. You have to have something else to be conscious of. This is the beginning of the split mind.
- From the book The Disappearance of the Universe by Gary R. Renard [5.1]

The viewer and view screen must stand apart in order for the viewer to view the screen, not physically apart, but there is a sense of *space* in mind. It´s like a mirror. In order to see yourself and be aware of yourself you need a reflection - a mirror - the sense of something apart from you the viewer.

Also, consciousness requires time because it needs to recognize whatever it is viewing. Re-cognition is view and acknowledgement like bouncing a ball off a wall. It is feedback and that takes *time*. Consciousness is achieved via a feedback loop of re-cognized thought. There is an essential and demonstrable element of space-time in the mind. Not physical per se as the mind is not a physical entity, but it's still apparent all the same.

Space and time are the same thing, quantifications, but from different perspectives. One seen and one experienced. Time is tied to space. The viewing of the mind, seen as re-cognition, takes a modicum of time; it's a feedback loop, view and acknowledgment. Outward view and returning re-cognition. Therefore consciousness or self-awareness is tied to space-time. It is not possible outside of the space-time mechanism. Consciousness needs a space-time construct to exist. For God to be aware of itself space-time is required, *but* God is infinite - The Mind that forces a finite realm into existence in order to experience itself - it's potential. But how can this God have knowledge of Himself prior to creation of the finite? How can that be? How can God - The Mind - know that it is All That Is if there is no finite space-time construct to allow for awareness of that fact? Consciousness requires space-time and space-time is a finite construct. Space-time can´t exist in the infinite because the infinite can´t be quantified and known. It is an unknowable state. There is no time in the infinite. Hence consciousness can´t exist in the infinite and still God is aware of his potential (or knowing) in the Infinite? How can God - The Cosmic Mind - be aware and know of its potential while being infinite? *This is The Paradox.*

Consciousness requires the finite realm of space-time, but at the same time consciousness can´t logically end, and it can´t be quantified. So consciousness also exists in the infinite as potential, unlimited - un-manifested consciousness. This is the knowing - the concept not yet realized. The Mind is both finite and infinite. This is the big mystery of creation. It is *The Paradox of Creation*. The confusion of the actual paradox comes via a mass misconception of what the infinite actually is. The infinite is an unknowable state. We will never understand infinity. It can´t be understood. It can´t be measured. It can´t be quantified.

Anything defined is simply an aspect of the "potential" all and note also that quantification has to be supported via time-space, so it's as if the infinite potential feeds into the time-space bubble. To know is to quantify. As in that you can know the answer to the sum, what is $1 + 1$, you can conclude the question as in that it resolves as 2. How then can you 'know' the infinite? How can it be quantified? It can´t. It is unknowable because it can't be quantified and no, you can't know bits of it, anything known is defined manifest. Anything known is finite.

THE TEACHINGS OF SRI NISARGADATTA MAHARAJ

The Indian spiritual teacher and philosopher Sri Nisargadatta Maharaj (1897 – 1981) explained the finite/infinite aspect of creation like this:

If you try to understand the un-manifested with the mind, you at once go beyond the mind, like when you stir the fire with a wooden stick, you burn the stick. Use the mind to investigate the manifested. Be like the chick that pecks at the shell.

Speculating about life outside the shell would have been of little use to it, but pecking at the shell breaks the shell from within and liberates the chick. Similarly, break the mind from within by investigation and exposure of its contradictions and absurdities. The longing to break the shell comes from the un-manifested. [2]

As such the infinite, "the life outside the shell", is a mystery. It is the Magic. The finite is the logic. Logic is used to understand and explain the space-time construct - the finite, but it can´t explain the infinite. It is Magic. Magic begins where logic ends.

Creation itself is a paradox when we try to figure it out using just logic. Indeed logic concedes that there can be no logical origin.

This paradox is also apparent in the teachings of Sri Nisargadatta Maharaj where he talks about four stages or states of creation where the three first ones are just temporary:

Stage 1: *You are your thoughts, emotions, feelings, associations,*

184

memories, perceptions and body sensations.

Stage 2: *The non-verbal I AM.*
In this stage you no longer are dependent on your thoughts, emotions, feelings, associations, memories, perceptions and body sensations to know who you are so you enter into the next stage - the non-verbal I AM.

Stage 3: *Pure Consciousness.*
You enter into this stage when you realize that you are not The I Am - that this too is a temporary stage. You are pure consciousness and everything is a "bi-product" of that consciousness.

Stage 4: *The Absolute Nothingness.*
This is the final stage and it comes after the realization that consciousness itself is temporary. This stage is PRIOR to consciousness. It is The Absolute Nothingness.

Consciousness appears on the Absolute and we are all rays of the Absolute
- Sri Nisargadatta Maharaj [10]

Again we see that time is involved. If something is *prior* to consciousness time is involved. If Consciousness *appears* on the Absolute time is involved. Prior to when? When did consciousness appear? Time can't exist in the Absolute Nothingness because this is the Infinite. The Infinite is an unknowable state where time and space cannot exist. Hence *creation is a paradox.* There is no "actual" awareness in the infinite, but it has to include consciousness as consciousness is apparent, and so part of the infinite "all" as there is no origin. So what is, always has been, "no thing comes from nothing", so what is "is".

With the crux of the paradox being that if consciousness does exist, then it has to re-cognize, and so it forces a time-space bubble in order to facilitate and realize itself. Here you

185

can see how something can "seem" to come from nothing. It's, metaphorically speaking, that consciousness is a seed within the infinite that can't help but grow as it HAS to manifest.

The actual paradox is that The Mind - The Absolute Nothingness - is infinite and yet conscious of itself being All That Is, and consciousness is a tide to time space and therefore finite. As such creation is both logic and magic, but current science doesn't understand that. They claim that it is possible to answer the question of creation purely within the realm of science, and without invoking any divine being, a God - the magic.

As Steve says: "Why can God be referred to as magical? Well, if you are following this logically, you can see the un-manifest as the infinite that contains the finite that will expand, so yes there is no need for God in that sense. The paradox itself perpetuates existence. However, why does anything exist at all? The infinite may not need a linear origin as time does not pass from that perspective. But it is an *is-ness*, as opposed to an *is-not-ness*, which would have had to remain an *is-not-ness*. Why is there an is-ness, and there you have magic! Because there is no possible reason, the reason would require a reason."

Science only uses logic and logic alone will never solve the mystery of creation. It´s like science is the chick speculating about life outside the shell. First, they have to realize we exist within the shell and that the shell is a construct for creation in order to experience who we are. There's nothing - no thing out there! All the 'things' are in here in the egg, in the bubble, the manifest. We have to reach a point where the way forward is via an extension of logic, a knowing of what logic actually is, using it as a tool instead of being a slave to it. We must use logic to view The Mind from within like the chick breaks the shell - from within. Logic in itself will never give the big picture. Science has tried to find a unification theory via logic and they fail over and over. They fall at the first hurdle actually as in how did the Universe logically begin, and all they can come up with is a bang for no reason which is in no way logical.

Science has been able to trace the creation of the Universe back to approximately 13.7 billion years ago. They know what happened a billionth of a second after the Big Bang and forward to our present time. But they don´t know what happened before this billionth of a second. Why? Because they use logic. Logic ends where magic begins. They say creation must have come out of nothing, but there is *no action in nothing*. They seem obsessed with finding an answer to creation without a creator so they come up with their own definitions of nothing - a nothing complying with the laws of physics. It seems like they are slaves to logic and fail to see it as a tool for understanding our space-time construct - the finite world.

There is no point in speculating about life 'outside the shell'as Nisargadatta Maharaj puts it. They want to use logic to know it all - to replicate the Big Bang to find answers to creation and maybe even go beyond the boundaries of the finite - beyond the Big Bang. They spend billions of dollars to build one of the biggest machines in the world (The Large Hadron Collider, Cern Switzerland) to replicate the Big Bang - to see how energy turns into matter. Science just doesn´t get it. There is a creator - an intelligent design behind creation - and magic (the infinite) begins where logic (the finite) ends.

THE SLEEPING MIND

It is difficult to try to think in terms of finite and infinite. We have to separate the concepts in order to understand in a linear way, but The Mind is both. Logic and Magic. All is Mind. When The Mind loses it's space-time element, when it can´t feedback and re-cognize itself, it 'sleeps.' Sleep and wake are achieved via The Mind oscillating from the two contractive states - Infinite and Finite.

Most people think that infinity is really big, but really big is a size. They say that the Universe is infinite because it is ever expanding, but ever expanding is also a size and thus just part of the finite. That means that the Universe we live in can´t be infinite. It is finite. Our planet Earth sits "in space". If the Universe was infinite we would not be sitting 'in space' because 'sitting in space' means sitting inside a boundary - like being inside a gigantic balloon, but where is the balloon?

If the Universe is infinite how can we be 'in space' if space cannot contain a logical boundary to be within? The infinite has no boundaries. As such the space-time construct, our Universe, is finite, but then *where are the boundaries?* If we could reach it, bang on it, then we would have to ask, what is on the other side? Why are we 'in here», in this 'bubble?' What's outside the 'bubble?' A boundary in space would not be a logical end to space or a logical end to anything. It would pose the question 'What's beyond it?' In truth the Universe is not physical, it's like your mind, a bubble that can be as big as you like.

Man can´t reach the end because man is an aspect of The Cosmic Mind and therefore always in the middle. As far as man can travel there will be space. The boundary will never be found because all is Mind.

Logic is nothing more than our format, indeed the format of consciousness which is a feedback loop, it is all circuits. It is created via fragmentation and reassembly, a cosmic game. It´s like a jigsaw puzzle with all the pieces scattered around and the game is to put it back together and the tool we use is logic. Therefore what is explained above can be seen as a greater logic that better describes the illogical infinite. The infinite is un-manifest. There is no time from the infinite perspective because time is a measurement - quantification. The infinite can't be quantified in any way. So there is no time passing and no space. A yet that does not mean that it does not exist, hence the analogy of a sleeping mind that can't recognize itself, can't experience the "passing" of time, and yet it exists outside of time passing.

As stated above the actual paradox is that The Mind is infinite and yet conscious, and consciousness is tide to space-time and therefore finite. Since The Mind is part finite and conscious, space-time is "forced" into being in order to facilitate the said consciousness. Therefore a space-time bubble explodes (The Big Bang) out of the static infinite to then allow for the finite conscious element to exist. A finite realm 'is created.' *Consciousness facilitates itself.* The Mind sets up the construct for consciousness to experience itself. The infinite forces the finite into being through a Big Bang event - space and time appears out of *No Thing* turning energy into matter forming eventually this incredible universe. This nothingness science is talking about is not nothing. It is the infinite part of The Mind forcing the finite into being so it can experience itself. It needs a Waked State to be aware of itself. It is the abstract, un-manifested potential becoming a concrete manifested reality. In fact The Mind is both The Sleep Mind and The Waked Mind - it´s only *One* Mind. The Universe 'kick starts' due to the nature of consciousness, which demands and forces space-time in order to facilitate itself. However there is no starting point to the Waked Mind - to the finite realm of space-time.

It is part of The Mind with no origin - no starting point. The Big Bang event seems like a starting point when seen from our space-time perspective, but in truth this too is Mind.

All is Mind and The Mind is both still and moving at the same time - The Paradox! Infinite = Still =no time passing. Finite = Moving = time passing.

The infinite is potential consciousness - un-manifest - and it can never exist in space-time since that would be to quantify it and the infinite can´t be quantified. It is an unknowable state. In order to experience the potential that lies in infinite potential consciousness, a space-time environment (bubble) must be in place allowing for consciousness to experience itself in all different shapes and forms - to live out its potential. How would you know what things feel like if you don´t experience them? Being by doing is the solution.

The space-time bubble that is in place due to the criteria of the conscious element is a finite, "limited", linear reflection of the infinite. In order to be known and experienced as it has to be to then allow for consciousness to exist via re-cognition, it plays out in a linear way. It is a linear logical story format, this so that it can be understood which is to know. The Mind is facilitating itself using a bubble in which it can manifest and experience. As such the finite world is created and anything that has a start (the Big Bang) must also end - law of logic. It ´s like 5+5 = ……..if we don´t provide the answer there is no logic. It only concludes when the solution is given = 10 - quest solved. It makes sense when it is solved.

The infinite/finite paradox is God - it is the alpha omega - *all* and *nothing* (no thing), but this No Thing is actually infinite potential consciousness - the concept - the knowing that is longing for experience.

God is in everything in our finite world, and God is also the infinite, the potential that is not yet manifested - the abstract that wants to be concrete and physical. All is The Mind of God and The Mind has created an unstoppable chain reaction, an ever recurring cycle so there is no true beginning.

The infinite is not no-thing - it´s more like a sleeping Mind - sleeping because there is no space-time element to then allow for the conscious re-cognition of the waked state. The viewer and the view screen aspects are one in the same - non place - no feedback. This can then be seen as the state of the Universe, un-manifest, prior to the Big Bang. It is not nothing. It is simply un-manifest. Nothing is something and something is nothing.

The Mind exists and yet it does not re-cognize so it is potentially anything, and yet beyond the linear format of space-time it can´t be known. When the Mind is awake in the finite it creates and enjoys the awareness of it because there is re-cognition of self through experience.

SOUL ASPECTS

In order to explore the creation and experience process in the finite realm God has to interact so it splits into soul aspects. Without interaction there would not be much of an exploration of what consciousness may manifest as. There is only One, but being One is being alone. Many spiritual people say that we are all one like cells in a cosmic body. Yes, we are soul aspects for the One to experience itself - to interact. However, All *One* = *Alone*. The One splits itself into many so it would not be all alone and unloved. That's the only reason we are here.

Creation is a reaction to the core truth of oneness. In order to interact we, the soul aspects, have to think we are individuals - we have to forget we are God. Forget so we can re-member. God created spiritual aspects of Himself to know Himself as God, but in order for the souls to know of themselves as God they would first need to know of themselves as Not God *and* experience it. Hence the souls have to forget before they start playing the game of life. It´s like a jigsaw puzzle. When the pieces are scattered all over the reassembly process begins. We can´t see the complete picture so using the tool of logic we start putting the pieces together. As such we as souls must forget we are God. If we knew every single piece of the puzzle and in what order to put them - it would not be much of an experience.

We need to forget and then the creation and experience process can begin. Basically we have to believe that we are real or we wouldn't play, and if there is no play then the conscious aspect can't facilitate itself and so there would be no consciousness. And the truth is that we as aspects are not real as such but more reel as we are ever recurring. In truth there is only one of us here. So we have to hide. The jigsaw puzzle picture is being created from the scattered pieces using logic as the tool: *One piece here and one piece there. This one is not fitting with that one - let´s try another one.* This is doing - this is experiencing. The creation process or assembly of the jigsaw puzzle is in its way resulting in getting to know the puzzle. Experiencing, really knowing, requires a world of polarity - of duality - of opposites. For example - how can you understand if a piece of the puzzle is big or not if you have never experienced what small is.

For God to be known the soul aspects need to think they are individuals, they need to forget they are God *and* they need to experience duality - experience opposites. Why? Because the world of duality - of polarity - of opposites is the tool we need to experience ourselves and to really know who we are.

Taken to ultimate logic, you cannot experience yourself as what you are until you've encountered what you are not. This is the purpose of the theory of relativity, and all physical life. It is by that which you are not that you yourself are defined. [4]

How can you experience warmth if you haven´t experienced cold? How can you know what pleasure is if you haven´t felt pain? How will you know, appreciate and feel love if you haven't experienced fear? Hence the need for this 3D duality world we call Earth where we come back over and over again to play out different characters. All the lives we have experienced are part of a greater cycle of our soul. This cycle is in place to enable us to fully experience duality. We have experienced what it's like to be male and female, healthy and ill, rich and poor, 'good' and 'bad', villain and hero, a king and a servant, a teacher and a student, a warrior and a pacifist, a killer and a savior and so on. We have been at this game forever. We have been playing out all the characters you can imagine. This dualistic world is created to help us know who we really are - who God is. There is only One Mind and this Mind has infinite, un-manifested potential consciousness. Within this potential there is a dualistic potential containing the male and female parts.

This is further explained in one of the channeled messages from Jeshua through the medium Pamela Kribbe. Jeshua represents the Christ consciousness who speaks through many since the time has come to wake up to who we really are. Christ consciousness can be seen as the part of the mind that knows and re-members God. And as we are all One Mind then we all have potential Christ consciousness.

The Christ energy stems from a collective energy that has gone beyond the world of duality. This means that it recognizes the opposites of good and bad, light and dark, giving and taking, as the aspects of one and the same energy and from this energy springs the male and female:

The male energy is the aspect that is outwardly focused. It is that part of God or Spirit that drives outward manifestation, which makes Spirit materialize and take form. The male energy therefore knows a strong creative force. It is natural to the male energy to be highly focused and

193

goal-oriented. In this manner the male energy creates individuality. The male energy allows you to separate yourself from the One, from the Whole and to stand alone and be a specific individual. The female energy is the energy of Home. It is the energy of the Primal Source, the flowing Light, pure Being. It is the energy that has not yet manifested the inner aspect of things. The female energy is all encompassing and oceanic; it does not differentiate or individualize. Now, imagine the energy of the female becoming aware of a certain movement inside of her, a slight restlessness, a desire for... reaching out, outside of her boundaries, moving outside of herself to attain experience. There is a longing for something new, for adventure! And then an energy comes to her that answers that longing. It is the male energy that wants to be of service and help her manifest in matter, in form. The male energy defines and shapes the female energy and by their cooperation the total sum of energies can take a completely new direction. A new reality can be created in which everything can be explored and experienced, in ever changing forms of manifestation. [11]

This is the Big Bang where the finite realm 'is created'- where consciousness facilitates itself in order to manifest No Thing into Some Thing – Every Thing. In *The Disappearance of the Universe* Gary R. Renard says everything that would seemingly occur was already set in motion in that instant of the Big Bang:

It's true that The Big Bang symbolizes separation. On the level of form it was so tremendous it rendered an unfathomable force of energy. This in turn predetermined all physical laws and the fate of every cell and molecule how each one would evolve and which direction they would go in. When we say the movie has already been filmed we are saying that everything that would seemingly occur was already set in motion at that instant and in fact couldn't really occur in any other way. All the different dimensions and scenarios are simply symbolic of different big bangs within The Big Bang that occurred at the same instant. [5.1]

The Big Bang created a bubble of space and time including both space-time and time-space with all the different realities we can experience. It´s like the infinite is fertile soil and something within the soil is moving about wanting to get out. A seed wanting to break the surface of the infinite and spring into the finite world to grow and stretch. The Infinite has within it The Primal Source - home - pure being - unlimited potential not yet manifested, but also the longing to attain experience of this potential. This leads to The Finite realm - the male energy that can separate from The One - from the Whole and be a specific individual. As such a space-time construct 'is created' to facilitate this manifestation. The cycles of creation and manifestation are driven by the core paradox of the infinite and finite - the Primal Source longing for outward manifestation. It is The God Force - Shakti - in action. Shakti (from Sanskrit shak, 'to be able»), meaning sacred force or empowerment. God - the shakti - is un-manifest because it is paradoxical. The moment anything manifests it will be dual - female/male. Complete circuits including both poles to allow feedback! What is hot? The opposite of cold.

We are here to create and experience and in that know ourselves - and in the process we re-member who we truly are. God created many souls in order to know Himself. Man is created in the image of God, but in order for man to be more than just a creation, man has to possess individual consciousness. These are the soul aspects using the human body as a vehicle to manifest potential consciousness as form in the finite space-time construct.

We all come from the same pool (the infinite) and each droplet of this pool can be frozen and defined as a form in the finite space-time construct just as a character in a movie. We come from the same Source, but still we are unique. When we loop back to Source after the experience of finding out Who We Are it´s like we are melting and looping back into the pool - once again joining it. Pool - looP. This pool - God - has always existed - the infinite without any starting point or end point - no time - no space. But why? Why do we exist?

WHY DO WE EXIST AT ALL?

Bashar, who is an energy entity channeled by Darryl Anka, has given his answer to this question. Mr. Anka is an internationally known channeler, speaker and author. In 1983 he began to communicate, and trance-channel messages from Bashar. When asked the question Why do we exist at all? Bashar answered as follows:

Because you have to. Existence simply IS. The question "why does existence exist?" is a question created within existence. The question is subject to existence. Existence is not subject to the question. Existence only has one quality - to exist. Therefore that which exists simply exists. It doesn't in any way, shape or form need to justify its existence by asking why does it exists. Existence exists because that is the quality it exhibits: existence. [12]

The Infinite Mind just *is* (no awareness) and when the question *"Why do we exist at all?"* appears it must appear from within the space-time construct - the finite - The Waked Conscious Mind. The part that is aware. When we, as soul aspects, are within the finite space-time construct we, (The Mind), become aware that we exist. Consciousness requires the re-cognized feedback loop, space and time, to be aware and hence the question only arises since we are conscious, but we don't re-member who we are so we ask the question. When The Mind is infinite it can't ask questions - it's not self-aware - it is only a potential. We simply exist.

The One Mind - The Mind of God has always existed because there is no such thing as an ultimate logical origin. This drives a logical mind crazy because the logical, linear mind needs a resolution, and a starting point - a why? It needs to conclude - 2 + 2 = 4. It can´t be satisfied with 2 +2 =......? The quest is not solved. That's open ended, abstract. This is because we are part logic and part magic. The Infinite/ Finite Mind - The Paradox of The Mind - a sleeping unaware Mind and a waked, self-aware Mind. It is a great cycle of cosmic sleep and wake.

The Paradox Point is the core - the in-between state where the finite and the infinite touch - almost "intersect". When consciousness experience itself in the finite it can get close to the core and still be aware as my friend Steve did. He went to the core in extreme slow motion in order to see what actually happens when you die or fall asleep, lose consciousness; it's the same thing really. This so he could understand the life cycle and then accept God. How many souls have experienced this core as Steve did? Every single soul experiences the core when they leave the physical body and die, but they pass through it so quickly that they don't see what happens.

Steve is the first one I have met who has experienced this Paradox Point and can describe it. I have worked with and met many shamans, mediums, psychics, channelers and people with near-death experiences and none of them have ever mentioned the core. According to Steve they would definitely talk about it if they had an awareness and a memory of it, because the impact is beyond what anyone can imagine. It sticks with you because it has an incredible strong and lasting effect.

However, many speak about experiencing bliss, heaven, The Kingdom, nirvana, unconditional love, euphoria. Yes, because simply by leaving the manifest world you feel euphoria.

As you move towards the core the sense of joy, love and freedom makes you want to cry. It´s is like there is an orgasmic rush on the way in to the

core. Like an orgasm, but in your mind, your whole being. It's nearly too much to bare.
- Steve Berg

The closer you get to the core the more you sense the oneness and the love intensifies. There´s only one of us here and getting closer to the core make you realize that you are one with everything. You are it. Together we all make up the cosmic body called God since we are like cells in a cosmic body doing, creating and making it possible for us *to be*. As such the love confirms the oneness of it all.

People who have been 'on the other side' have felt this intense, unconditional love, but none of the people I met had experienced getting really close to the core as Steve did. It seemed like he experienced going all the way through 'different layers of The Mind' and get as close to The Paradox Point as possible. It seems like he went 'further' than all the others. His experience shows that it is possible to be really close to the infinite and still be aware, but eventually you black out because the infinite can´t be understood, viewed or experienced - there is no awareness there. Of course you black out because as you return to the infinite, see it all and become it all, you join with it and lose your feedback loop, so you become un-aware! It´s like when you fall asleep each night. You will never be able to pinpoint the exact time you fell asleep and moved into the unconscious, unaware state. At some point your consciousness drifts away - you become unconscious - you fall asleep.

Every night we are doing the exact same thing as The Cosmic Mind is doing, and yet in micro fractal. We move from The Waked to the Sleep Mind - from the conscious to the unconscious - from the aware to the unaware - from the finite to the infinite. We do it on a smaller time scale than The

Cosmic Mind. As above so below. We go through this wake and sleep cycle every night and the only difference from The Mind of God is that we don´t forget our linear path when we wake up the next morning. Why? Because we are part of The Mind of God and we must continue the cycle, but when the cycle ends - when the Cosmic Waked Mind falls "asleep" - when it is putting in the last piece of the puzzle it forgets. That's the big crunch! Consciousness falls only to rise again. The puzzle is complete and we must start over again - scatter the pieces all over once more so we can put them back together again. There is nothing more to re-member so we must once again forget - fall to rise.

WE FALL TO RISE

The Mind - God - we as soul aspects of God - sleep and wake, we fall and rise again. We forget in order to once again re-member. The fall is the fall that happens in consciousness. Many spiritual people talk about the fall in consciousness after Atlantis.

So did the sleeping prophet Edgar Cayce:

The inhabitants of Atlantis possessed a deep understanding of the forces operating in the universe and the fact that they could use them to create their own reality. However, they abused their power over nature. Because they chose an egotistical and materialistic path, thus causing a set-back in human evolution.......

This misuse brought on the destruction of our great cultures and a long, karmic soul journey through the pain and confusion that resulted from our selfishness and self-centered focus on our will without regard for the will of the Creator and others. [13]

Another view of this is that no-thing, lasts forever. We are now approaching the part of the story of the exploration of consciousness where we now begin to slowly wake to this truth. We will shift in consciousness to a new less limited reflected reality. We will experience the Mind via a less limited format and really see what this 'thing' can do! We will eventually consume all experience, become complacent, and that's when it's time to reboot. This is the *fall* we go through in order to once again rise. We have been on a long journey back to a higher consciousness. We forgot in order to re-member and now we are starting to re-member again.

As souls we exist in the space-time construct - in The Waking Mind and we all pass through the core every night when we sleep - when we shift back to the infinite state of un-re-cognized sleep, but it happens so quick we don't notice it. You can't remember the exact moment you fall asleep, how can you? On a larger scale this is what The Cosmic Mind does too - it goes through the great cycle of cosmic sleep and wake. As above, so below.

Steve has explained to me how he experienced the actual mechanism of the mind passing from finite to infinite. He lost space-time, the linear, as his past and future reeled in as external time condensed. Leaving only the space-time element in his own mind, this allowing him to re-cognize, be aware. He's says he became singular, that he touched the All, God was showing him the cycle!

As in microcosm so in macrocosm. The concept was later laid out in The Emerald Tablet of Hermes Trismegistus, in the words "That which is Below corresponds to that which is Above, and that which is Above, corresponds to that which is Below, to accomplish the miracles of the One Thing. [14]
- Source: Wikipedia

Is this how creation works? A cycle of a sleeping and a waked

Mind? Splitting itself into fragments to experience itself in the finite while still being infinite? A paradoxical Mind? We live in a world where science is the truth provider and we want proof before we can believe. We rely on science to tell us what is true. However science is using logic to explain creation, but logic is only really a set of inevitabilities in place in order to create a format to then allow consciousness to play out interactive scenarios that then allow us to experience consciousness, as in it's infinite abstract form it is .....nothing - No Thing - yet. Yes, logic is a game, an eternal game. We are simply consciousness, the finite manifest is a tool, a construct, a vent in place so we may be conscious via a reflected format, but we need interaction.

If we say that God is *all*, then in order to 'be' it separates into Adam, the logical defined finite realm, and Eve, which is another representation of God - the undefined, the unlimited. In God they both already exist. Men then are of Adam, of logic and in this finite linear, logically space-time construct we experience time - past, present and future. Hence we gain a *history* - the history of logic - of Adam - *His-story*. Women are of Eve, who is more like God - the mystery - *Miss-story*. Of course from the macro view in that analogy we are all of Adam, Eve is never seen. This including manifest women, who yes resemble the infinite in their 'way', but then both men and women are of the manifest. And each containing male and female traits to a degree.

The Big Bang was an explosion that saw energy transform into matter to then create a Universe of spinning bodies that can be inhabited to then allow for His-story to play out. Creation is a story format. Logic. Miss-Story is the mystery part - not of logic - the undefined, the unlimited part that can´t be seen or measured. This is why women tend to be more intuitive.

For the last 400 years man has been occupied with what can be seen and verified. Man has been occupied with logic.

Why? It started when René Decartes back in the 16th century split body from mind and soul. Since then science has looked to matter to explain creation. Matter became the main focus. 'Matter is all that matters.' Some years after Decartes split the body from mind and soul Sir Isaac Newton came along and described the physical laws. His discoveries led to an understanding of a Universe working just like a clock - precise and with tiny parts interacting. It became known as the The Clockwork Universe Theory.

It´s all about matter - the visible world. Not the unseen - the un-manifested, but rather the seen - manifested world. But then it has to be noted that Newton was genuine Mystic! He was indeed searching for God via science, forced to conceal his esoteric writings. Science is trying to explain creation by looking at matter, but they don´t realize that the thing that creates matter is consciousness and we are part of that consciousness. We tend to place ourselves outside of creation of which we are an inseparable part and unit.

As Deepak Chopra says:

The greatest mystery of existence is existence itself. There is the existence of the Universe and there is the existence of the awareness of existence of the Universe. Were it not for this awareness, even if the Universe existed as an external reality, we would not be aware of its existence, so it would for all practical purpose not exist. Traditional science assumes, for the most part, that an objective observer independent reality exists; the Universe, stars, galaxies, sun, moon and earth would still be there if no one was looking.

However, modern quantum theory, the most successful of all scientific creations of the human mind, disagrees. The properties of a particle, quantum theory tells us, do not even exist until an observation takes place. Quantum theory disagrees with traditional, Newtonian physics.

Most scientists, although respecting quantum theory, do not follow its implications. The result is a kind of schizophrenia between what scientists believe and what they practice. When we examine this hypothesis of traditional science, we find it more a metaphysical assumption than a scientific assertion. [15]

CONSCIOUSNESS CREATES

If traditional science is correct then energy came out of nothing to then create matter, which eventually created a life form, called human beings who are conscious. This implies that matter created consciousness. Is this correct? No, it´s the other way around. Indeed Steve points to the CODE that reveals this. Why a Code? Well everything in some way resembles the All as there is nothing else to copy. The fractal effect! Therefore, everything is intrinsically encrypted. If you take the word CODE in upper case, turn it upside down, and look at it in the mirror, it still says CODE. It's one of the only words in the English language to do that. It's trying to show that everything is upside-down and back to front. Mind is all, the physical is the illusion. This 'reflective' CODE then extends into the rest of the English language via multiple meanings of the same word, as in whole and hole. But then you won't spot the CODE if you don't know the cycle, as in real and reel, it means nothing outside the context of the cycle as in that the 'real 'is really a reel, a cycle.

Words such as form and from, again opposites showing self-creation. What is seen as formed is actually from. Or the word knowledge, which breaks down into no-ledge as there is no tangible root to any of this. In truth there is no ledge. So, consciousness created matter. Consciousness has always been here and consciousness is forming our Universe second by second. Since we are part of this consciousness we (God) create our own reality moment by moment.

Consciousness is creating and consciousness needs the space-time construct to be aware of its own creations. Why would we otherwise need to think and be conscious before we create anything today? We are thinking beings - conscious beings living in a space-time construct - the very parameters needed for consciousness to be aware of itself. Thought is an attribute of consciousness, the filter through which consciousness manifests itself into form.

Hence, any product or service a human being wants to create must first be a thought. We need to be conscious of what we want to create. It is *impossible* to create anything without thinking about it first. Just go ahead and try to create anything without first thinking of it and being conscious of it. It can't be done. The first car could not have been produced without Henry Ford first thinking and being conscious of how to create it. When he formed a clear picture of the car in his mind he started to create it. Consciousness creates form and matter - not the other way around like current science suggests.

This was understood by author Wallace Delois Wattles (1860 – 1911) all the way back in 1910 when he published his book *The Science of Getting Rich*. Prior to publishing this book he had been studying various religious beliefs and philosophies of the world including those of Descartes, Spinoza, Leibnitz, Schopenhauer, Emerson, and others. Through his tireless study and experimentation he discovered the truth of New Thought principles and put them into practice in his own life. He began to write books outlining these principles. He practiced the technique of creative visualization and as his daughter Florence relates:

He wrote almost constantly. It was then that he formed his mental picture. He saw himself as a successful writer, a personality of power, an advancing man, and he began to work toward the realization of this vision. He lived every page ... His life was truly the powerful life. [16]

In his book *The Science of Getting Rich* he refers to *The Formless Substance - The Formless Intelligence* from which all is created:

There is a thinking stuff from which all things are made, and which, in its original state, permeates, penetrates, and fills the interspaces of the Universe. A thought, in this substance, produces the thing that is imaged by the thought. Man can form things in his thought, and, by impressing his thought upon formless substance, can cause the thing he thinks about to be created. [3]

The formless substance he is talking about is consciousness. Consciousness is permeating, penetrating and filling the interspaces of the Universe. Consciousness is what the Universe, the space-time construct, is made of. In the finite realm - in our Universe - consciousness creates through us - through you and me. We are part of The Mind making us believe we are conscious, thinking beings with a human body when all is actual Mind. It is an *illusion* - a *hologram* reflecting the potential of God.

In *The Disappearance of the Universe* author Gary R. Renard also touch upon this:

Reality is invisible and anything that can be perceived or observed in any way, even measured scientifically, is an illusion - just the opposite of what the world thinks. [5.1]

However some physicists are beginning to grasp this. They say that this hologram is something that could be a valid theory for how our world exists. They call the theory The

Holographic Principle. We live inside this hologram - this space-time construct. We experience life. We are like characters in a movie manifesting God´s potential. The unseen, un-manifested comes alive and experiences through us and in that God can really know Himself.

In this movie the human body is used as a vehicle for consciousness. The bodies are electromagnetic by nature. The biology is electromagnetic and the brain and the heart are big electromagnetic field producing organs. Hence our thoughts and feelings are actually specific electromagnetic units influencing atoms which make up the so-called reality.

Back in 1972 Jane Roberts (1929 – 1984) wrote about the electromagnetic attributes of thoughts and feelings. Jane Roberts was an American author, poet, psychic and spirit medium. She said she 'channeled' a personality who called itelf *Seth*. Here is an excerpt from her channeled book *Seth Speaks* published in 1972:

You do not realize that you create your larger environment and the physical world as you know it by propelling your thoughts and emotions into matter. Each of you acts as transformers, unconsciously, automatically transforming highly sophisticated electromagnetic units into physical objects. You are in the middle of a matter-concentrated system. Each thought and emotion spontaneously exists as a simple or complex electromagnetic unit, unperceived, incidentally, as yet by your scientists. [17]

Wallace D. Wattles says the same thing using other words:

A thought, in this substance, produces the thing that is imaged by the thought. [3]

In other words, whatever we think about will be created. However, in order for it to be created the thought must be strong and steadfast. Thoughts are energy and as Einstein realized energy can become matter: $e=mc^2$, but it requires a lot of energy before it becomes matter. It´s like snowflakes. In order to make a snowball you would need thousands of snowflakes. Using just one snowflake doesn´t quite cut it. It´s the same with creating from the formless substance - it requires a strong and steadfast thought. Thinking the thought just once is the same as using one snowflake to create a snowball. It´s not going to manifest into matter. Keep thinking the same thought over and over and over again. 'Let it snow.' In other words you must really believe you can attain whatever you want and put your heart into it because this will produce a strong impact on the formless substance.

Thoughts and feelings are electromagnetic units influencing our physical world - shaping it. With faith and purpose you will be able to create whatever you want. This is consciousness in action. The infinite, un-manifested potential experiencing itself in the finite world. As Wattles says:

Your part is to intelligently formulate your desire for the things which make for a larger life and to get these desires arranged into a coherent whole; and then to impress this Whole Desire upon the Formless Substance, which has the power and the will to bring you what you want. You do not make this impression by repeating strings of words; you make it by holding the vision with unshakable PURPOSE to attain it, and with steadfast FAITH that you do attain it. [3]

The Bible says: *Man is created in the image of God.* Consciousness created a conscious life form in the physical, finite world called human beings. These are characters in the movie who are conscious and thus have the ability to think and feel. Hence, we, as human beings, have the same power to create as the consciousness that created us. We are all part of this consciousness - The Mind of God, and there is no limit to what we can create *if* we believe we can do it. As Jesus said:

Truly, truly, I say to you, whoever believes in me will also do the works that I do; and greater works than these will he do, because I am going to the Father.

He says: whoever believes in me will also do the works that I do; - What does it mean? My take on it is this: if you believe that we are all part of the creator - part of consciousness - God in Disguise- we can create whatever we want like Jesus did. Thoughts become things and you can create incredible work (matter) if you produce enough energy.

It is all about having faith and purpose as Wallace discovered. Just look what Mahatma Gandhi did. What he did seems impossible. How did a skinny, little man like Gandhi manage to remove the British Empire from India using non-violence? He *believed* with all his heart that it could be done. He impressed his thoughts upon formless substance and shaped his own reality - a reality where India was free. He got his fellow countrymen to share his belief. When people gather and have the same intention it is the greatest power in the Universe.

Anything is possible for those who believe. When you believe in something you are saturating your cells with this belief and that sets up a certain vibration which your cells emit. This vibrational signal emits into the Universe - the sea of consciousness - and is basically saying: "I want this to be created" - and through the Laws of The Universe (Law of Vibration, Attraction etc.) it will be created.

The Mind is *all knowing* - all the inventions that the world will ever see have already been invented. Who every connects with All That Is in a strong and powerful way will be 'granted' access to 'this part' of The Mind and can bring these inventions into the physical world. The formless substance, consciousness, creates - through you and me, in the physical Universe we see. Anything can be created like Jesus and other Ascended Masters throughout history have discovered.

This is how infinite potential consciousness can experience itself in the finite world - through you and me and through every atom that exists. My friend Steve has a slightly different take on the phenomenon of manifesting, the law of attraction. He says that we are as characters already complete from the greater perspective. Therefore we are following the role of what would be seen as our higher complete self. The small self can't manifest as it doesn't have the overview. That's like a character in a novel starting to go off on its own tangent based on its current perspective, which is only part way through the book. Manifesting, as it has come to be known is then an alignment of the character and its role, they want the same thing. However, if you want what is not in the book then you will go wanting.

In order for consciousness to play out its potential the jigsaw puzzle starts in the finite world. The Big Bang occurs. It is the urge to experience the physical - to manifest. The result is the realization and manifestation of the infinite potential of God in the Universe we live in. In the finite world The Mind is Awake and can be aware. Also, the awareness of itself comes through conscious beings like us, human beings. We are aware of the Universe. We are conscious. We are God in Disguise because man was created in the image of God and God had to forget in order to experience Himself. All Is Mind so we are inside The Mind of God acting like separate conscious beings and we are aware of the Universe in order to gain experience - the abstract becoming the concrete - the potential manifesting in the finite.

We are points of consciousness within God´s Mind and The Mind has created an incredible thought-based Universe as a playground for us souls to explore, through different life forms, to manifest its potential.

We are all rays of the Absolute.
- Sri Nisargadatta Maharaj

When we are born we arrive with this potential. We can become and express anything our heart desires. It is our gift to the Earth, to the world. We all have this great potential within and the gift is what we manifest - what we create and share. By doing this we gain experience helping us find out who we really are. Being by Doing. God gains experience and lives out its potential. But then how can we manifest what is not written? How can we change what already is?

Steve explains it like this: You are already a complete character from the overview. The character and its role, its journey are one. Therefore what will come for that character is based on who he or she is, and therefore the character naturally fulfills itself! When you resonate with certain ideas and dreams and create from your heart you are most likely fulfilling your role. We are here to express our unique role and when we die we can look back and see what we did with the great potential we were born with. Did we let it all out? Did we die empty by manifesting the ideas and dreams within us? or did we die full - full of potential - talent, ideas, dreams and uniqueness that never saw the light of day? In other words did we consciously align with our role? With our part in the play? What are the gifts we leave behind - what did we do with this life time? Did we live out the potential and die empty? Or did we just go through life conforming to the masses? Did we let fear get to us so we died full - full of ideas and dreams that never saw the light of day? Our regrets are part of who we are. So where does that leave you?

Back at square one, you simply play your life the way you, the character sees fit, and to the best of your ability, what else can you do? And in the end, how it went down was inevitable, so no, ultimately no regrets from the macro view as the micro regrets are part of the experience. So try not to worry.......but you will....or you wouldn't care and you wouldn't be playing a part.

The set-up is simple - manifest the potential - the uniqueness. We bring with us the gift of this potential and we leave behind whatever we did with this potential - the character we played. Creation is all about experiencing life - manifesting ideas and dreams and enjoying the process. The journey is the destination there is no goal. Create - produce - cause to exist. But where do the ideas come from? They come from the God inside - the Higher Self guiding us so we can play our part in the game - be the character in the movie. You wouldn´t 'get'an idea if you lacked the power to manifest it. You get an idea suitable for your part - your character. That´s why we are all different. Can two people 'get' the same idea? Yes, but the implementation and the manifestation of it will be unique for each one.

STARTING OVER AGAIN

Here we are - experiencing creation in our unique way in this finite world until all is experienced - all is consumed. It´s like watching a movie. You enjoy it while it lasts, but it has to end - so too does this experience we are part of. As time goes by conscious beings like humans start to gather more and more pieces of the puzzle and re-member that we are in fact part of this consciousness - that we are God in Disguise.

We are getting closer and closer to completing this phase of the puzzle. We experience everything in the finite world - understand and re-member more and more until there is no more to experience. It has all been done. The conscious aspect of The One Mind has re-membered and consumed all that can be consumed in terms of experience around a premise.

What is next? And what happens when "the whole movie ends"? It starts all over again. Why? Because the conscious aspect of the Mind can´t ever stop re-cognizing - it must stay conscious. The base conscious aspect of The One Mind never ever sleeps - it is itself 'wake.'

We, as souls aspects, pass through wake and sleep, but from the greater view wake and sleep are constant states, they "are". If the conscious aspect of The One Mind ever slept, became un-manifest, became infinite, then what would wake it? There is no re-cognition in the infinite. It may as well be seen for all intents and purposes nothing - no-thing. No action, no recognition. It has no need to manifest. It is asleep - unaware.

If we see the wake and sleep as on and off, then some part of The Mind has to stay *on*. Why? Because the infinite is *off* and if The Mind is off who will turn it back on again? The *on* is and so it constantly blows bubbles. There is only One Mind. It´s just like a PC. If you turn it off, then it can't turn itself back on again, so it only ever goes into standby mode and that's not a real *off*.

It´s like the smashing of a puzzle to put it back together again. All the pieces are scattered all over and the puzzle needs to be reassembled. The smashing of the puzzle can be seen as the Big Bang event where the space-time construct is created for consciousness to re-cognize itself. Then the assembly begins using logic.

Logic is self-contained in the space-time bubble - in the puzzle - since it can´t explain anything beyond space-time. Logic is the framework for re-cognition. It is the tool being used to explain life and creation. Piece after piece is being put together - the puzzle is slowly being reassembled. It uses the linear format with time past, present and future, so it looks like evolution. It makes sense - *this goes here and that goes there*. It is a logical puzzle-based space-time bubble that serves as a vent away from the unknowable infinite where consciousness can exist.

When consciousness has consumed and grasped everything in the finite realm - when the puzzle is finally assembled it gets stuck. There's nothing left to re-cognize! What now? And what more is there to do - to find out - to solve - to experience - to create? It needs to do something to experience itself - to be self-aware. Only then can it be something - being by doing. It has to interact to explore itself so it splits into soul aspects.

When The Mind, through these soul aspects, has re-membered and experience all there is to experience in the finite realm it does not stop, indeed cannot stop re-cognizing, and so it turns to the only "other" than itself - the infinite. It attempts to quantify and view its infinite aspect - the finite and the infinite attempt to join. The linear loops back, the circuit that should be so large it seems to be a line loops back in The Mind of God and joins itself, Bang. This creates an acute paradox point, like a short circuit because the finite and the infinite as opposites can´t join- they cancel each other out. Nothing can be its own defining opposite. You can't be hot and cold, or in and out, not in the same perspective.

If the finite becomes infinite - if it slept - went into off, it will lose its space-time element, the viewer and view-screen aspects will condense to become one in the same and therefore it can't feedback and re-cognize. Therefore it becomes un-self-ware, it will sleep - turned off and then it can ´t turn itself on again. When The Paradox Point is reached where the space-time logic bubble has been consumed, the positive and negative aspects of the paradoxical all touch, it short circuits at an impasse, and The One implodes and explodes, sleeps and forgets via fragmentation of The Cosmic Mind.

What does this look like symbolically? If the finite conscious aspect becomes infinite then its viewer and view-screen aspects that feedback and re-cognize, condense into One, it implodes. On the other hand if a finite view point tries to view and quantify the infinite, all it would ever see is endlessly expanding space, it explodes. But then Implode/ explodes to where? There is no other than it, it can't be lost. Therefore the fragmentation can be seen as the metaphoric smashing of the space-time bubble puzzle, to then allow for the continued linear reassembly process, that itself is time - space-time. It takes time to solve the puzzle. If we solved the puzzle there is nothing more to do and so no time (no movement).

In other words The Singular Mind explodes in order to forget and alleviate the paradox of not being able to move. So the whole become the hole. The further out on the explosion the more fragmented it is. Which means that you have to link all the fragments in order to see the whole and those fragments can be seen as the knowledge of The Mind that we are and play out. The more fragmented The Mind is, the more time there is. In the same way that the more fragmented a jigsaw puzzle is, the more time it takes to assemble (re-member) and when the puzzle once again is complete we smash it and start over again. It is the fall in consciousness - Adam bites the apple. God breathing in and out - the bouncing universe - an infinitely repeated cycle of universal expansion and contraction.

What is being smashed and fragmented is The Cosmic

Mind since it is All That Is. The Mind of God. God is paradoxically all, but destroys Himself in order to re-member Himself and 'be' via the remembrance. We are God. We are the puzzle. We are that which is lost and found. As the Hopis say: *We are the ones we are waiting for.*

God through us had to forget in order to reassemble the puzzle once more. When we start to re-member we are beginning to see the whole picture. Each time The Cosmic Mind falls - each time the puzzle is smashed into pieces - it forgets what it is. This to then allow for the "journey" of reassembly to seem to be new. This has to be the case as The Mind has to seem to be linear or it doesn't make sense. So it runs in logic cycles. The endless is illogical it can't be understood and as Steve says, "You can't stand under what you can't understand". When it finally feeds back, fully re-members at The Paradox Point, the circuit completes, it becomes circular not linear.

That's why it cancels itself out, and makes no sense. Add here the concept that beyond the fragmentation that allows us to feel real. The mind actually created itself, which means it's a figment of its own imagination, and that renders the mind insane, which is also why it loses cohesion on seeing the whole truth. It loses sanity and it takes sanity and stability, which is logic, in order to recognize. It reverts to its infinite state, which intrinsically does not "make sense" - it simply is.

In forgetting and re-membering a limited finite version of All That is, The Mind can be endlessly self-aware which it has to be because the infinite is a constant. It never ends, or begins for that matter. It *is*. It simply *is* - still - not moving, a constant.

The world has never been at all. Eternity remains a constant state.

- From The Disappearance Of The Universe by Gary R. Renard [5.1]

Movement (time) is needed for The Mind to be conscious and awake. If it just is - if it is still there is no movement - no time - no feedback loop for recognition. As such the finite, wake part of The Mind has no choice but to loop back on itself as it has to keep moving seemingly forwards, and yet there is only a finite amount of reflective matter. It begins around a logical premise that has to conclude or it would be open ended and then random and in that un-re-cognizable.

THE RIDE

The Mind wants to create experience and manifest its potential and is using the space-time construct to do just that, but creation is not really in a linear format. It only appears to be. We are floating along in the river of time. What's behind us is the past and what's in front of us is the future, but from

The Mind's perspective all moments coexist, like all of the pages of a book or frames of a movie. They are all there, but when you read a book you only read one page at the time. When you watch a movie it is shown to you frame by frame. As such you can see all life in front of you like a book you are about to read or a movie you are about to watch.

Creation can also be seen as a ride you are about to embark upon. You get on and you look forward to this exciting ride. You think you haven't been on this ride before so it's all a 'new' experience due to the Mind fragmenting in order to alleviate the paradox where it got stuck. Before you start the ride you have been 'wiped clean.' Consciousness fell and had to forget in order to re-member.

The Mind is No Thing at the moment it embarks on the ride. No Thing wants to be Some Thing. It wants to *be* and must create and experience for this to happen. We, as point of consciousness, embark on the ride. When we are loaded we react to the ride to then become a product of the ride. As we see more of the ride we *become more* of what it is making us be.

The ride is changing us as we ride, grow, re-member - it's a loop. Re-membering and growing would feel much the same, but we are re-membering. In the linear we are travelling the circuit endlessly. The ride is powered by the commutator (the infinite) which switches our polarity from full to empty so we can keep going round the same thing. The commutator, the same as in an electric motor, the rotating switch that continually changes polarity in order to keep the motor moving.

The infinite explodes/implodes the finite on contact, which is The Paradox Point. It can be seen as a giant magnet that wipes our minds like a magnet wipes recording tape at the point where the last piece of the puzzle goes in. On the way to this point (the end/beginning) the ride keeps rolling and we never leave it no matter what level you think you are on. The level is only really dictated by the reflection of the stage your mind is at on the cycle. If feels like we are growing, but we're not, we are re-membering a cycle on tracks.

The ride is a circle or actually a spiral that ends up where it started, because it leaves the infinite and returns to it for re-wiping. The end is the beginning something Gary R. Renard also mention *The Disappearance Of The Universe*. He is actually quoting *A Course in Miracles* which says: *the beginning and the end - which are the alpha and the omega - are really the same thing......For where the beginning is, the end will be.* [5.1]

The closer we get to this end/beginning point - The Paradox Point - on our ride the faster it goes. On our way back to re-memberance we are moving along a spiral because the more we travel around, the more we know, which means it's a decaying orbit. The more we re-member the closer we move to the core - to The Paradox Point. It's a geometric process because the more pieces of the puzzle you have completed the less time it takes to complete the rest of the puzzle.

But then also try to understand here that when the Big Bang occurred, no 'one' was here. The universe then reflected the absolute fragmentation to the point of forgetting, and so it looked empty. Gradually the explosion/implosion cooled off, the paradox was alleviated so it was no longer reactive. This symbolic mind then started to come back together very slowly, relatively speaking. Elements formed as it re-membered, then planets and then as it re-membered more fundamental life appeared leading to evolution which is obviously following a design. Natural selection makes no sense as many scientists are beginning to realize via numerous examples.

Indeed if life began via certain amino acids and proteins colliding in a primordial swamp, a chance in a million that science states as fact and yet can't recreate. Then what are the odds of this accidental life being able to procreate, let alone thrive? But then the point I would like to shed light upon here is that each soul will enter and exit the metaphoric stage as needed. Each soul will live over lifetimes and levels playing its parts, but then when it's not needed anymore on the greater cycle it's shelved until the next loop. So no, we don't all end up in the core. Indeed Steve suggests that his core experience was only in order to extend our knowledge so that the cycle can turn. This so we can stand under a new less limited reflected reality.

Each soul weaves its way through the greater cycle. The spiral tightens exponentially and the spiral is nothing more than a manifest symbol for the shape of The Re-membering Mind - a tightening spiral with a singularity in the middle. It´s like water going down a kitchen sink drain. The rotation increases speed as it drains. In a draining tank, the water by the drain has the least momentum. As it leaves, the remaining water with more momentum takes its place. If an object moves closer to the center of its rotation, it speeds up. So, the water gradually picks up speed. This is what is happening with our ride. We are the object moving closer to the core by re-membering more and more. Things are speeding up and this is exactly what Terence Kemp McKenna (1946 - 2000) talked about in his Time Wave Zero Theory.

McKenna was a writer, public speaker and philosopher. He developed a program in the mid-1970s and called it Time Wave Zero. Time Wave Zero is a numerological formula that purports to show different events in time, defined as an increase in the Universe's interconnectedness. According to McKenna the Universe will increase its ability to make connections. Everything will speed up and the Universe will reach a singularity at which point anything and everything imaginable will occur instantaneously. Time will cease to exist.

This fits very well with The Paradox Point as described in this book. When time cease to exist there is no movement and with no movement (no space-time construct) there is no consciousness - no reflection. The Finite meets the Infinite - the in-between point - The Paradox Point and here The Mind (us as soul aspects, fragments) gets wiped. We forget. Consciousness falls in order to rise again. Another Big Bang. It has to keep going to be awake (finite). It can´t fall asleep (be part of the infinite) because who will wake it again? There is only One Mind.

Eventually we reach the end which is the same as the beginning, the circuit completes and you end up back at the constant infinite where there is no time, as if you never left, and remember that 'time' never even happened from that perspective. The ride keeps going and going. It never stops or leaves, it just gets wiped and carries on as the end is the beginning again. Like a carousel never stopping.

The dimensions or levels we go through are part of the ride. It's really just part of the one ride, like that we are a baby, child, teenager, adult, middle aged and old in one life line. The infinite isn't part of the model other than it's symbolically the invisible electricity that drives it, the magic and the commutator that switches polarity. As you pass through the core - The Paradox Point - when the last piece of the puzzle goes in - it wipes The Wake Mind. Consciousness falls - forgets - and then off we go to another round. The Sleep is where we forget to re-member.

If life is an equation that unfolds like an onion with many layers and levels, then *Sleep - peelS* the onion. As the ride is moving along more and more is being 'peeled away' and we slowly wake up re-membering who we are.

WALKING AROUND THE GLOBE

The ride is one way to illustrate The Paradox and how our past is actually our future. Another one is the 'walking around the globe' example. Imagine you decide to embark on an exciting adventure by walking around the globe. You decided to walk around the globe at the equator level. Each step you take will leave a mark in the ground as you walk along the equator. It will be your unique marks - what you leave behind. At some distance in front of you there is a machine clearing the path. As such the path will seem clear and fresh to you. Each footstep will leave a fresh mark. You are not able to see the machine ahead of you. As you walk along the path it will seem like a brand new path - never been walked upon, but the more you walk the more you start to re-member this path.

The path changes you. It changes how you look at yourself and who you are. The path ahead of you will represent your future and the path you have walked will be your past. You would seem to walk straight ahead all the time in a linear fashion, but you are actually walking around the globe - on a circle. The reason you don´t see it is because the circle is really big. Your perception will be that of the linear view, but in reality you are walking along a circle and you will end up where you started. Your path ahead will actually be the past since you are starting another round. You have walked this path before, but as you reach this starting/ending point (The Paradox Point) you fully re-member and The Mind gets wiped (re-boots - sleeps - forgets) and once again you seem to be starting out on a fresh, brand new path. Again note here that indeed some souls will never ever reach enlightenment. If it's not necessary for their character, you 'die' on the cycle simply when your personal mini-movie is complete. And you don't have to see the paradox in order to die and reboot, anymore than you have to see it every time your mind loses cohesion when you fall asleep, it happens too fast. Again which is why Steve had to see it in slow motion, up close and personal, in order to understand and extend the cycle. We all come and go on cue. Therefore Steve actually died in slow motion. Well, experienced what death really is and lived to tell the tale.

This is the 'game' God is playing. A never-ending game -

hence the need to forget. It's the same with a movie you have seen. From the emotional aspect you can't watch the same movie forever, you would go mad. You would go 'around the bend'- you would go 'loopy», and seeing as there is only one movie in town, one infinite, that we can't renew - we have to forget in order to re-member. We renew, we ourselves recycle, we don't live and die, we sleep and wake, forget to re-member. It's like God "told" Neal Donald Walsch in *Conversations with God:*

There is nothing else to do.....this is the only game in town.....The only question is whether you'll be doing it consciously, or unconsciously. [4]

Most people don't see this game. We start 'a new movie'- 'a new walk around the globe'- 'a new game' so we can play again, but without remembering. We are playing it unconsciously. This is the game we all play - infinite potential realizing itself in the finite. We play out this game through different characters. It's all part of the construct to allow the infinite potential to experience itself in the finite. This is why we need to forget in order to re-member. Consciousness needs to continue in the finite world and the whole thing starts over again. It's like watching a movie. Once you finished the movie you wouldn't want to see it again straight away. You wouldn't want to see it for a long time because you would remember the characters, the story, the ending. Maybe a year later you had forgotten the story and you would watch it again. Watching the same movie over and over again would be boring and eventually it would turn you crazy.

Just like Bill Murrey in the movie Groundhog Day from 1993. The character Phil wakes up to find that he is reliving February 2nd. The day plays out exactly as it did before, with no one else aware of the time loop, and only Phil aware of past events. For Phil the day is boring because he knows exactly what is going to happen. He has relived the same day over and over again. No element of 'new'-same old stuff. Hence, we need to forget to enjoy. Forgetting is part of the "set-up" in order to play the game. If you want to enjoy a movie you have seen before it would be best if you have forgotten most of the story and how it ends. As you watch the movie you start to re-member more and more of the story, the characters and what comes next. You are re-membering. It´s the same with The Movie of Life.

This Movie of Life keeps playing and when it reaches the end it starts all over again. We keep re-playing it with all the different characters it contains. This is the reason we are all unique - it allows for many characters and interaction within the play. More to experience. In her book *We Live Forever*, author and an expert on near-death experiences, P.M.H. Atwater is certain that we all come here to play the game of life. She says:

I know as an absolute truth that every single one of us has a part to play in life´s drama. It is important that we play our part with all the heart and soul we can muster. It is no accident that we walk the earth for earth is God´s gift to us - the stage on which we act out our many roles as we change, grow, transform. Actually, the whole Universe is our playground.
5

All is Mind and we are part of this Mind playing the game, but in order for The Mind to be aware of the game and all the characters it has to re-cognize its reflection. At base it's thought, but in reality, our reflection is the Universe. The Mind has to re-cognize in order to be conscious, but then as it is All That Is it has to recognize itself, but what is it? Simply consciousness and it has to do something in order to be something - that evokes the souls, soul aspects. You can't do much by yourself - that´s not much of an exploration of what consciousness may manifest as. In order to interact the soul aspects have to think they are individuals.

Note here a very profound truth that everyone always harps on about when they speak of God. When they ask why it has to be so bad here. Somehow we have to taste the bitter in order to define the sweet, and therefore someone has to create that bitter, therefore some aspects have to play the bad guys! It´s part of the interaction set-up. We need the full 'cast of characters.' You can't play yourself at chess. If you are both players then you know 'the other guys' strategy and in that the game comes down to a series of inevitable offensive and defensive moves, but then how do the souls appear to be different? Why are they not clones? Individuality is achieved via subtraction.

The one soul would be all knowing and if you cloned it then the copies would think in the same way as the one soul, a kind of telepathy that is not a connection per se, just extreme like mindedness. And in that there would be no valid interaction, everyone would agree!

Even though All is Mind you might say that the souls are the only real thing here. How? They are real because they are the I's of God. We are all *the eyes - I´s -* of God in that we are God in Disguise, but we don´t re-member so we think we are the body, the person, the character we play in this movie.

You are not the person you are - not the "I".
- Sri Nisargadatta Maharaj

If you are still attached to your religion, your color, or the country you were born in, then you still don't know who you are.
- Prince Hanuman

As souls we are here to express life - to create and experience life. We are here to manifest the un-manifested infinite potential. The sleeping prophet and psychic Edgar Cayce also spoke of the soul aspects and how they came into being. Below is an excerpt from John Van Auken's book, *Reincarnation: Born Again and Again* based on Cayce readings:

According to the secret teachings, there came a point in this creation where the Creator's Consciousness desired to bring forth companions, creatures like unto Itself that would share in this expression of life. In order for the creatures to be more than creations, they had to possess individual consciousness and freedom so that they could choose to be companions. Otherwise, they would only have been servants of the Original Consciousness. So within the One Universal Consciousness many individual points of consciousness were awakened and given freedom. [18]

Souls possess *individual* consciousness so we may interact and experience, teacher and pupil scenarios, entertainer and audience etc. We lack so that we may be given, which is interaction, an experience of consciousness playing with itself. God, the remote intelligence that runs the program, makes us what we are. We are like characters in a play, type casted.

We all come here to play out our part. To create ourselves anew. That´s the goal, if there is a goal - the goal of facilitating consciousness? So if God wants you to play a part then you will be given what you need in order to play that part. This is your life purpose. Your soul contract. When you are on 'your path' playing your part you are given divine guidance and help, because it will add to the total experience. It´s like a puzzle and we are all unique pieces. You have to fill your place in order for the puzzle to be complete.

We all play this game and we all must play our part for maximum experience in order to be. If we don´t, we are not filling our place in the puzzle and the puzzle is not complete. We are all God in Disguise - and as such God is hiding from Himself in order to experience the infinite potential - to manifest the un-manifest. God, through each and everyone of us, must forget in order to re-member. We don´t live and die. We sleep and wake, we forget to re-member. This is the game - this is creation.

The core is the key. Think of it as one miraculous Mind floating in nowhere and what it would take for that Mind to feel 'real», to believe it was real, feel the wind on its face when it has no real face. It has to fragment into soul perspectives and load into a supporting program so it can interact. It has to forget its own truth in order to be part of 'reality'- the space-time construct. It has to tie itself (time - tie me) to this 'reality' or the experience won't stick. It has to experience every defining opposite of the things it wants to experience. As such we as soul aspects are carrying out this experience. We are God in Disguise. However, if The Mind tie itself to this 'reality' where is the freedom? How can we be free? In truth The Mind is nothing *and* eternal. In order to feel free *it has* to be tied to this program - the time-space construct - in order to seem to choose freedom. And yet if it leaves this program, it is nothing. Being free from the program makes no sense. Free to be what? Nothing - the No Thing. It's The Paradox from another perspective. The Mind *needs this reality* - this construct in order to be something, a format. Floating in 'the system' is fine, but you can't 'live there», there's nothing to 'do'. In 'that place' we are No Thing - the un-manifested potential wanting to manifest - to be Something.

Ironically, paradoxically, we have to be tied in order to be free and there's another code, tied and tide, ebb and flow! As such we need this game. Since All Is Mind what we perceive as our reality is all a construct - a program. Everything is symbolic, we have no real base, no real limitation. The limitation only comes when we introduce the premise. Technology, logic? We use logic to try to figure out who we are and where we come from, when we in fact are only consciousness. We don't come from any 'place'- we are consciousness.

We are God in Disguise and God is unlimited potential wanting to experience the finite realm. God is the potential that wants to manifest - wants to give since the essence of God is pure Shakti - a sacred force able to give - pure love. It is always there just like our hearts beat independently of our knowing. The heart of God is pure Shakti, pure love, which is why it beats, to be able to experience that love. God has been waiting for us to come home. God misses us as much as we miss God. We are on our way back home to Oneness.

From the heart we are able to connect with others and transcend ourselves. The heart transcends the boundaries of the ego and enables us to feel oneness with anything outside of ourselves, even with All That Is - with God. As such the heart chakra is the gateway to the energy of Home. Our time on Earth now is about to become a conscious co-creator creating from the heart and not from the ego. This for the safe souls who can experience the 'power' of the unlimited force that we are without hurting others. If the greedy ones could manifest, this world would break out into a cosmic war! Which is why we are contained when we are 'young», as in life, children need rules and guidance.

God is 'live' defined via the beating of the heart. God is an over product of the constantly beating heart like you are alive because of your heart, and we are that heart, the cycle, the pump. But God does not live like we do, God is not linear on a loop, God is the endless line - infinity - eternal, because God is driven only by love, whereas we are driven to live and experience in the finite realm. At base it's All Mind - God is driven by love and we are driven to live it out. Love makes eternity work. God - the unlimited potential lives to give since the only way love works is by giving it. We come to this space-time construct with the gift of this potential and to manifest it into our reality - to bring it forth in our 3D Earth.

God (Love) divided itself in order to know itself. God wanted to give and receive, but being alone - The One Mind - it had to split in order to know this love. And of course if God is love, then it has to be concealed in order to be revealed, which answers many questions as to suffering. Within the potential of this Mind there is a dualistic potential containing the male and female parts - in other words it is dualistic in nature. Looking at this as a linear story The One wanted to love and be loved - a two way street. A feedback loop, but The One had nothing to love or be loved by, so it split into two, hence the symbolic tail of Adam and Eve. They needed a place to enact, to facilitate their love, and as such the world was created with many, many copies of Adam and Eve - the soul aspects - the fractal effect.

Or put in another way - love is an energy that endlessly gives. It has momentum and the momentum has to go somewhere. Why does it have momentum? Because it is conscious and consciousness as movement has to go some 'where'- hence the space-time construct where we come to live out the potential - the love - the joy, but that evokes fear and pain in order to define the said love and joy. Love is always there - the glue that holds everything together, but when we reach the last piece of the puzzle - when we come to the end of the cycle (the finite world) then God has nothing left to love other than God (the infinite) and this is The Paradox Point resulting in God 'killing his baby'- the space-time construct - the puzzle is being smashed.

The Cosmic Mind falls in consciousness and out of the

'dead baby 'grows a new tree of life, a new 'baby' to love and give to. This so that God can carry on loving - not feeling alone, and we can carry on living, we live - God loves. God´s love flows like our lives flow, and it all backs up at the paradox point. God is the giving force and love is more of a constant thing, even when we are really in love time seems to stand still. We come to this Earth plane to manifest the unlimited potential of God´s love and it all starts with the Big Bang. The story goes that life evolved on Earth, and that always plays out the same way, so The Mind is remembering the story and it condenses into characters only when it "reaches that part of the story". At a certain part of the cycle back to oneness human beings evolve - The Mind re-members more - and we play out our part of the movie. Another frame is being revealed.

Characters like human beings are created and formed (form-from) by the Earth since the Earth can be seen as the heart of God - as the pump that forms characters. Earth-Hearth. The earth is the heart. (Do you see the earth in heart?) Once you have been through Mother Earth, you are real. It´s like we, as souls, come through the pump (the earth-heart) and are formatted and grounded to then go out into the abstract body until we are depleted and then come back to the pump.

To be re-formatted. God is Shakti - the sacred force- and it needs 'containers' to enter into in order to define itself. As such 'containers'- characters in the movie - have to be created in the story. So Shakti then fills all 'containers.' It creates 'containers' via the story. It creates characters. In other words the heart creates definition so we can see what we are in a reflective way. We are The One and that One has to escape oneness somehow in order to be, it has to create the separation of time-space. The finite within the In**Finite.**

229

All is Mind and when we leave this Earth - this 3D reality - we continue our journey in other realties and they are like copies of this one. Imagine a Word document or a PowerPoint file. The first document you make is the original one and from that one you can use the 'Save As' function to create copies. Using a PC analogy the finite world is the PC always ON and it uses software programs to create documents (realities). The Infinite is the power that runs the PC - always there making sure the PC is On. They need each other - the power and the PC - the infinite and the finite. The Yin-Yang.

The Mind uses the 'Save as' function and creates other realities. It copies itself. It is the Fractal effect. In these realities we can go back and forward in time. We are not 'dragged along' by time as in our 3D reality. Time ties us down, but in the other copies (realities) we can move about in time. We can 'bend the rules' so to speak, but these are not real universes, they are just copies. No one 'lives' in them. Everyone 'lives' here. It's a play and 'learn' tool. It shows you how everything is connected, meet great people, and see what color dinosaurs are. See who built the pyramids and so on.

You get to see how the whole story plays out. Why? Because beyond this 3D reality we become multidimensional and in that we become more aware of the connection to The Whole Mind - the whole story - the whole movie. In these other realities there is a great deal of fun and joy - no pain since we have paid in here. Pain = Pay in. We pay in here so we don´t have to experience pain 'there'- in the other realities of The Mind.

The story is a play that leads to the awakening, all connected, so you can take a better look at the book when you get out. We could spend years figuring it all out and have a lot of fun along the way, no hurry. All the

plots and subplots, we could see the crucifixion of Jesus, find out what really happened. We could watch all the people go by, doing all that stuff that they think is real, that you thought was real. All this is possible via God, God can do anything, except solve a paradox......no one can solve a paradox.
- *Steve Berg*

The Mind is always on 'the move.' It can't be still. Stillness - no passing of time - is the infinite and in the infinite The Mind is nothing - no awareness - no recognition - no consciousness. As such it moves along the cycle and into other realities, but it can never "stay there" on a permanent basis. When we die we get out of this 3D reality and sense oneness so we understand more of the whole story - the whole movie. No pain. We experience love and bliss, but even though these realities are more fun - have more pleasure and love we will eventually get bored and this allows for the ego to grow. When that happens The Mind shifts again - moving further along the cycle - never being still. So there is no Heavenly end station where we "stay forever", but it's one of the last stages of the cycle so we do get to experience it, but not stay there forever.

All is Mind and The Mind creates a system to experience itself. As such The Earth - the 3D reality- is the 'real' world where we come to live and finally realize the oneness of this Mind. We come here to test our spiritual ideals to see if they are real as the famous psychic Edgar Cayce - The sleeping prophet also touched upon in one of his readings. [29]

This world is a very dense world - heavy energy. It takes a long time to manifest anything here. A lot of time must pass from an idea is born until it is manifested in our 3D reality. Why? Because we are supposed to enjoy the slow process of manifestation. Being aware of this process moment by moment - being present - is what God wants through us. To love every second of it. To love all the aspects of the manifestation process - all the interactions with other people until the idea is a reality. This is experiencing, creating, doing and that leads to *being* which is what God wants. As such this world is 'the most real' world and it sure feels real. Of course none of it is real per se since all is Mind, but our world is like the original place - the master copy and that's why we seem to have very little freedom here since we are characters playing out our part in a movie. We have no say in the plot so to speak. Beyond this 3D reality we can play and 'learn' in unoccupied copies. It doesn't matter what goes 'wrong' in them.

This world is the actual heart of God. We are all real here, as real as we will ever be and it does indeed feel real. It formats us. Because it is real, it makes us real. You come to Earth and you believe you are the character, it sticks, and it gives you a good attitude for life, via the unavoidable negative experience. As such we learn (re-member) to appreciate everything and are considerate of others. After all - there is only one of us here - One Mind that has always existed.

There are not billions of minds in the world at all, but only one, and it is in everyone of us.
- U. S. Anderson

I once had the pleasure to talk to author and spiritual teacher Michelle Belanger who told me she remembers all her lives. I asked her where we go when we die and she answered: *You don't really go anywhere—you are in between spaces and you are one with everything.* I asked her when she was "born" as a soul and she answered: *I can only remember that I have always been.* Logically this doesn't make sense since we want a beginning. How can we always have existed? We have to see that logic is just the parameter of the construct. We are part magic and ultimately we simply exist. What is there to know? That there is nothing to know, everything is a game really, a game designed to bring love which unfortunately evokes fear in order to define the said love.

It takes a real keen intellect to realize that intellect is only a tool. You have to get serious to figure out how to stop taking things so seriously. The future is a leap from one perspective, but then a leap in the sense that things will be better by letting go and going back to what is. Less is more, but it takes more to figure that out.

This book provides an overview of the creation cycle from the infinite to the finite and back - over and over again - the only game in town. It is a tool to see the bigger picture and when we do we can let go of any fears and limitations we have. Life becomes easier since this reality - this game is a blessing for us to really be Some Thing. We are God in Disguise and in our space-time construct we are creating, experiencing and living out and manifesting the incredible potential of God. Outside this construct we are No Thing - nothing - just a potential not being realized - un-manifested. As such we need to forget who we are to experience ourselves (God). God chooses to hide in every created soul aspect who keeps coming back to the game - the program - the construct to interact and to experience every defining opposite of the things God wants to experience.

As representatives of God we are moving along the cycle of creation from a state of forgetting to fully remember. We don't live and die. We forget so we can remember. Consciousness fell only to rise again. More and more people seem to wake up now. More and more people question the way we live - a world with competition, unequal distribution and separation. More and more people understand that unity, cooperation and peace is the path to a better life for all. The ego must give way to the heart.

Many spiritual teachers tell us that the process of letting go of the ego and strengthening the actions from the heart is moving into a higher dimension of consciousness. They talk about going to a fifth dimension and becoming multi-dimensional. Moving into such a state is the same ascending. It doesn't necessarily mean that we will disappear from the earth. It means we can create heaven on earth. We can create a harmonic environment of peace and balance. When we raise our vibrations, we expand our consciousness and the cosmic mind opens up new rooms/compartments to explore. Once we realize that we are all one we leave behind duality, separation and competition and move into unity and harmony. We move from our ego to our heart. We realize that we are all connected. This is the shift in consciousness many spiritual teachers are talking about. This is where we are now - on the verge of turning into a multidimensional state. The Golden Age.

CHAPTER TEN

THE GOLDEN AGE

This time of awakening is about moving on. It´s about a shift in consciousness. This next level of reality is often being referred to as the fifth dimension. Is there anything indicating that this shift is ongoing? Yes, people sensitive to energies have for many years felt a shift in the energies coming into our atmosphere. The Earth moves through cycles and we are now being affected by these energy waves accompanying these cycles. According to author and speaker David Wilcock these cosmic waves are helping to change and activate parts of our DNA, which in turn is transforming our consciousness.[54]

A shift is upon us - a shift in The Cosmic Mind - The Mind of God. More and more people are waking up and starting to see and hear other realities. It´s part of the plan. We are moving along a cycle to experience ourselves and now we have come to a place on the cycle where more people are waking up and they are re-minding others. Yet another piece of the puzzle is being revealed. We start to re-member. Many experience a thinning of the veils between worlds which is expanding our awareness of the Divine. The curtain between the Earth plane and the spiritual world will eventually disappear and many will start to see and experience other realities (dimensions) created by The Mind. It´s like we are moving into another movie. Movies within movies, stories.

We are becoming multi-dimensional and in that we connect with other points of consciousness in The Mind. Some start channeling, others see, hear and become aware of deceased loved ones, and some see spirit guides and angels. Yet others see UFOs and so on. Are they all becoming crazy?

No, they are simply changing their frequencies. All is Mind and all the different realities are separated by level of frequencies. By raising your frequency you will be seeing and experiencing other realities created by The Mind. We are gaining access to other compartments of The Mind.

Since the frequency of your energy is rising it will parallel your level of awareness. A rise in your frequency is a rise in your awareness. You are expanding your consciousness. The point of consciousness you represent is widening its horizon and is becoming more aware of the whole - the other points of consciousness - all being The One Mind. This is being described in the book *Keys to Soul Evolution* by Jill Mara channeled from *Simion, Light Beings From the 7th Dimension*: -

As you reach into another reality, you also open a two-way valve so that your other self can, in turn, more accurately integrate various personality developments that you have made. You do not become each other. However, you share your consciousness more readily, and allow for a better understanding of who you are as a whole. [30]

PAIN = PAY IN

We can move further along the cycle now since we have experienced the pain that was needed in order to appreciate the joy. In this 3D reality we experience duality - polarity as part of the set-up. How can we appreciate being warm if we have never experienced being cold? How can we appreciate pleasure if we haven´t endured pain? We suffer pain - we pay in. It´s part of the set-up. We fall in order to rise. The next level of existence we go to has no duality. The joy 'there' is the result of the pain - pay in - here. There is no real pain there because we have paid here. So how much pain must we endure here before we can move on? How much suffering?

We need to understand that The Law of Cause and Effect is one of the Universal Laws in this space-time construct. You reap what you saw. When we appreciate life, even the painful moments, we expand our consciousness and understand that we are All One. This expansion of consciousness will reveal a new reality for us to experience - a reality where we create from the heart for the benefit of the whole - instead of creating from the ego for ourselves. When our frequency is higher and lighter we become more involved in creating with awareness. We become conscious co-creators and this process is on its way. Many are raising their frequencies now and starting to re-member that we truly are God in Disguise. The shift in consciousness is upon us.

THE SHIFT

The shift in consciousness many speak of is like a point at which question gives way to answer. It´s a point at which the Universe stops expanding, asking, and then begins to contract, answer, heal. We use logic to understand who we are. Logic is the tool in our finite world. It's our ability to problem solve, puzzle solve. It makes us feel capable, more aware and awake. It makes us feel bright, less stupid and dull. It lets us see more outside of us, understand more of the world we are looking at, and in that feel more aware, more self-aware as we can see more, feedback more. We feel like we are growing and learning, moving forward in mind which is part of re-membering.

Logic is getting us to a place where we realize we are also magic. We are becoming aware that we are multi-dimensional - that we are connected to all the other points of consciousness. We are The Mind. We are God in Disguise and God is All That Is - the seen and unseen - the manifested- finite world where logic is used as a tool - and the un-manifested - the infinite which can never be understood - it will always remain a mystery. As we move further along the cycle of life the more we re-member. We expand our consciousness and in that we perceive "new realities" - see more of the ride and re-member. Mother Earth is shifting her consciousness too. As beings of consciousness (points of consciousness) we are connected to everything also to the Earth and as such the Earth's transformation process will affect us as the medium Pamela Kribbe also has channeled in one of the messages from Jeshua:

The Earth is your house. Compare it to the house you live in. Imagine that it is being rebuilt. This will greatly affect your daily life. Depending on your state of mind, you will experience it as a welcome change or a disrupting and upsetting event. If you were planning and looking forward to rebuilding your house anyway, you are in sync with the changes and you can go with the flow. The Earth's transformation process will support and enhance your personal transformation process. If you did not want to have your house rebuilt at all, you will feel frustrated by the chaos surrounding you. The inner Earth changes will throw you off balance. For the ones who are welcoming the inner changes of your planet Earth, these will be extremely empowering times. You will be lifted by the wave of Light that is presently flooding your universe. At present, the Earth is almost cracking beneath the karmic burden of humanity. The negativity and violence which spring from this karmic burden form a kind of energetic waste that the Earth is hardly able to process, to neutralize or integrate. Focus your consciousness for a moment on the heart of the Earth. Relax and focus… can you feel something there? Can you feel how the Earth is being torn apart, how there is so much violence upon her? The Earth is feeling powerlessness and resistance at the same time. She is on the verge of creating a new foundation for her being. The Earth is going to release the energies of struggle, competition and drama, on inner and outer levels. The new foundation that is dawning within her is the energy of the heart, the energy of balance and connectedness: the living Christ energy. [56]

Yes, the new energy is the energy of the heart. Earth-Heart. We are transforming and shifting our consciousness because we are moving along a cycle of remembrance. This shift has started and we will eventually come to a part of the cycle where we experience bliss - what many call Heaven on Earth - The Kingdom. We 'stay there' enjoying and savoring these blissful moments, but the cycle moves on and in the end we will reach the beginning once again. It´s a cycle, but will all souls experience The Shift and then go all the way through all the cycle? Is this needed? After all there is only One of us here so is there a need for all soul aspects to move along the cycle? Steve explains it like this when we shift and go to a new reality:

We can now go to a new place where we don't die physically if we get run over or fall off a building. Because we are neither dead nor alive, it will be more like a lucid dream. We can extend the physical experience by not being physical, but we will still have limitation or we would get spoilt. Everything would get pointless too fast, we would be like the bored idle rich and that is no way to exist. All games need rules. In the next realms on the cycle the limitation slides....but those realms get smaller the closer you get to complete non limitation, which is? The core! Why do the realms get smaller? Because there's not much to do and experience there so you consume them faster. In these realms you do get absolutely spoilt, and this has to be experienced by some, so that The Mind can experience it, but it is the beginning of the end. And this is maybe confusing but, you can't have billions of unlimited beings that would be too many opposing wills all conflicting. Can you imagine if everyone on Earth had superpowers? It cancels itself out! In order to explore and play with these powers, you would have to split into smaller groups.

But none of this is physical. Think of it like reading the same book over and over. Some characters are killed off, but when you read it again there they are all shiny and new. Some characters are needed to lay down the premise; you can't start reading a book half way through, can you? You would ask, 'Well how did that get there?' And the answer would be 'Fred put it there.' 'Who is Fred?' 'Well if you had read from the beginning then you would know, but you don't need Fred now, the book has moved past his scene.' Where are all the dinosaurs? Where are the early monkey men? They were there in order to set the premise for us.

This is also something Gary R. Renard talks about in his book *The Disappearance of the Universe: The script seems to move faster and faster as time goes on, and your attention span gets shorter and shorter. Until you destroy your civilization and start all over again with little memory - like starting a new lifetime.* [5.1]

The book analogy is a good one since we are characters playing out a role on behalf of The One. In truth there is only one of us here - One Mind and The Mind is moving along the cycle playing this game in order *to be* and it uses different soul aspect to achieve this. As The Mind gets closer to the core (as it moves along the cycle or spiral) fewer soul aspects are needed. The whole creation process and the construction of this space-time/time-space bubble is for God to experience love - to feel love - not be alone. Love is the glue. Love tries to find itself, but some characters in the story, some soul aspects, are like cancer cells. They spread fear and are ego based. Yes, they are playing their parts in this duality world, but are they needed in the next realm - in the next phase of this cycle (spiral)? No, The Mind can do without these characters. It´s like turning another page in the book or another frame in the movie. The story don´t need them anymore.

So in a way love is leaving behind the hate, the greed, the negativity since it can do without it. In other words love is leaving fear behind, but then fear is born via the essential forgetting of God, so we can't avoid it, (ignorance). As such it is part of our duality world - our "part on the cycle", but now The Mind and the love can move on further along the cycle to the next phase. In the "next chapter of the book" or in the next realm fewer souls aspects are needed. All the extremely corrupted copies of The One will burn - fade away like characters that have done their job in the story. They are no longer needed.

How can that be? We must keep in mind that there is *only one of us here.* Fear through hate kills and every time a person gets an inflated ego it's another nail in the coffin (death). When ego rises love will leave. Each time we shift back towards the end/beginning or move along the cycle 'the survivors' will be grateful and appreciative this new reality for a while, but then they will soon forget and get bigheaded (ego) and that will force love to leave yet again. This happens all along the cycle - up all the levels of the spiral - all the way back to the core (paradox point) and when The One reaches this point, it creates a paradox which explodes The One descending back down to the start again - another Big Bang.

Why? Because the Wake Mind must always move - be awake. It can never stand still. Stillness - no time passing is the infinite and in the infinite we are nothing - no awareness - no consciousness. In our finite world nothing rests and this is why we can never 'stay in heaven' or stay any place on a permanent basis. It is a cycle - always moving from forgetting to remembering. From sleep to wake. The One forgets about being alone by moving along the cycle and this allows for a chance to love and be loved by 'others.' In a sense The Shift is happening because the ego has become too strong and it makes The Mind realize it´s time to go. This is exactly what the Mayans also talked about.

GREAT FORGETTING

The longest cycle in the Mayan calendar is 26,000 years and they divided it into five sub cycles. These were also further divided into 13 smaller cycles, known as the 13 Baktun Count, or the Long Count. Each baktun cycle is app. 394 years long, or 144,000 days. Each baktun was its own historical epoch or Age within The Great Creation Cycle, carrying a specific destiny for the evolution of those who incarnated in each baktun. We (Earth and everyone on Earth) are currently traveling through the 13th baktun cycle—the final period which started 1618 AD. This cycle is known both as *the triumph of materialism* and *the transformation of matter*. The Mayans predicted this final baktun would be a time of *great forgetting* in which we drift very far from our sense of oneness with nature and experience a collective amnesia. Like a memory virus in which we begin to believe the limited reality of appearances and grow dense to the spiritual essence which fuels this world, so *humanity's sense of ego and domination has grown*. They talk about the growing of the ego. This final period from 1618 until now is also the period where science has progressed and where *matter is all that matters*.

In the 16th century Rene Decartes split soul and mind from body and body (matter) became all that mattered. Science as truth provider number one excelled and we forgot about the mind and the soul. During the last 50 years we have seen an increased interest for the mind and now we see a growing interest in the spiritual. The last part - the soul - is emerging making us realize that we are body, mind and soul. Hence we start to re-member and it´s time for The Mind to move along to the next realm and leave the ego and fear behind. But why now - wasn´t the ego and the killing, the hate, the fear as strong in the past as it is now?

Looking back into the history of mankind we have seen horrific bloodshed. Hate and killing have ruled the world so why didn´t The Mind shift 'back then.' Why didn´t it move along the cycle and leave fear behind? The answer is that The Shift also includes all the knowledge that has to be known before any of this makes sense - can be understood. It´s like eating junk food and you don´t know it´s bad for you so you will keep eating it and eating it until someone finally shows you - tells you how bad it is. Then you shift your eating habits because you understand that junk food is not doing you any good. As such ignorance is to blame. In the past, we never had the language in order to understand this shift. Even now, with all the science, spiritual movies, books and teachers it is hard to grasp.

We don't realize that killing another is killing our self. We are like cells in a cosmic body and when The Mind through the soul aspects begin realizing this it will move on. And we are waking up and The Mind is shifting. It is moving along the cycle and at the end of the cycle The Mind fully remembers everything - all the tools of creation have been revealed. It has come to the last piece of the puzzle. At this stage The Mind is trying to find even more pieces. Pieces outside the finite world.

So The Mind tries to use logic to understand the infinite - the unknown part of The Mind - The Sleeping Mind - its 'other half'- the magic, but logic will never be able to explain the magic. So The Waked Mind must continue to keep itself awake and since there is nothing more to explore, create and experience it falls (sleeps/forgets) in order to start over again - in order "to move" - exist and be aware. The never ending game. The puzzle smashes into pieces once again and we start over. The Mind forgets in order to once more re-member. It has to. Since there is no more to re-member the only way is for consciousness to fall in order to rise again. It's like the seasons of the year.

We all long for the summer vacation. No work and all play. Sun and light all day long. Lazy days - bliss. However, being in bliss for too long will be boring. We want more and since we can't explore the infinite part of ourselves we fall in consciousness and forget. What comes after summer - the fall. We go back to 'work'- the 'holiday' is over - consciousness forgets to re-member and the cycle starts over. This is what the myth of Atlantis is all about.

ATLANTIS - THE KINGDOM

Consciousness fell - it had to in order to rise again. We had it all, but we were knocked out cold and now we are coming back around - beginning to re-member. We can see this remembrance in evolution, the logic of The Mind growing, returning and also in the way that more and more people are beginning to feel that there is something missing, something they forgot. We call it spirituality. People are beginning to feel that they are more than physical - more than their bodies. Spiritual movies, books, videos, seminars, webinars, forums etc. all talk about The Shift - stirring our memories - helping us re-member - more pieces being put together in the puzzle. We had it all on this plan-et. A wonderful place and so many 'others' to share it with. We thought we were 'real'. We believed the set-up - the game. We were not alone. Playing this never ending game is the way for The One to escape from being alone - it has so much love to give, but no-one to give it to. Yes, we are All One, but being one is being alone. *All One = Alone*.

Everything we call life, even the levels and dimensions, all of it, it never really happened because it is an illusion. You are The One, but by creating this game of life we can escape the chilling truth of being alone - we can give love and receive love. There *is* a way to be amongst others, and this life is it. We are it; we are the gift of life. We have each other. What a great gift. Atlantis is the symbol of The Kingdom where we had bliss, we had each other, and we had the tools to create the most spectacular things. We lived in an earthly paradise and look what we did. We destroyed our paradise as a result of greed - greed to know more - go beyond the last piece of the puzzle - to understand the infinite, but was it really destroyed because of greed? No, the whole thing was a set up - 'Adam bites the apple.' We fell so that we may rise again. We completed the puzzle to reassemble it once again.

We are God in Disguise - hiding from Himself - pretending that He is not alone with no purpose. It needs the finite space-time construct to give love, to know it self, to experience itself and forget the loneliness of being The Only One. God wants to give love and be loved and God is The One, and somehow, via magic and logic, The One speaks to us - screams and begs us from the core not to waste the gift of life - the gift of being here right now. God is love and God wants us to experience love in the finite world - our Universe - our playground which is in place to allow for God through us to feel love, but we have to suffer in order to define love. Of course when we are here, it all calms down to the extent that we take life for granted. We don´t see the bigger picture - that everything radiates from The One solitary soul in the core.

All of this space-time construct is in place in order for The One to have peace and love through us. Love is the best thing we have. What a wonderful feeling, but we need to share love. If we are only One there is no-one to share it with and this is why this game is a blessing. God - The Mind - is playing this ongoing game to feel *love* - to *be love*.

Love is the goal. Why? Because it's a reaction to the truth. The truth that we are alone, pointless and never seen. In that place what wouldn't you give just to hear someone say your name, let alone love you, want you, need you, give you purpose. Yes it's all about love and in order to know love you have to know fear. This game we play is the only game in town, but it´s a great game once we appreciate each other and love each other. We must appreciate all the *nows* in our lives. All the people we meet - the events - the circumstances coming into our lives. We came here to create and experience *life*. Right now we are within the construct of space and time and we have others to share our experience with. We are here

245

to enjoy the ride. We have others to engage in relationships with. We have people to love and people can love us back. We have the power to create and enjoy the nows of the manifestation process. This is our sole/soul purpose. We are not alone. We are experiencing the vastness of creation in this space-time reality. We must make the most of this gift. We must appreciate the Nows in life.

We are all getting ready for the New time awaiting us. The New Atlantis - the age of Wisdom of Creation. An age where manifestation will be shown in its fullest extent where we become conscious co-creators. It will create Heaven on Earth in an entirely new frequency. We have been waiting for this time for a long time - while going through the cycles of time. We have gone through many incarnations and built a solid foundation for this culmination of love and wisdom to be lifted in us.

The time is now for the old to be left behind and for the new to arise - like the snake shredding its skin. Our soul and spirit has been longing for this part of the cycle. After being in the dark and forgotten who we are, we are once again re-membering who we are. Deep inside there is a longing to move on to the next part of the cycle. This part involves re-membering that we are more than just our bodies. The longing is becoming stronger and stronger and more tools are given us to help us move along: crop circles with symbols, channeled messages and special drawings and symbols with sacred geometry, spiritual movies and books, music with certain frequencies, the dis-covery of hidden pyramids, The Language of Light and more people are seeing the veils disappear between our 3D physical world and the next level of the cycle. God - through us - is raising the level of consciousness to re-member.

We are carried along with the river of time and are moving into a new era to act out our part on a new stage. The infinite - the un-manifested is being manifested through us - through the parts we play. We all come from the same place - the infinite. It´s like we are all the same water, but then frozen and sculpted into different shapes. You can only be one shape, but it's all the same water, and water is a reflection of the infinite. It´s like we all come from the same pool of water into this space-time construct to create and experience as points of consciousness. In this reality we are tied to time - tie me - and thus we are like droplets from the pool being defined and frozen. It creates shapes to experience and then we loop back like rain always coming back to meet the sea. We loop from the pool: Pool - looP.

CREATING HEAVEN ON EARTH

Many talk about The Awakening - The Shift in Consciousness. The Hopis says: *We are the once we are waiting for.* It´s time to wake up. Spiritual teachers all over the world say the same thing. Waking up happens as part of the ride. We are on a cycle of remembrance. Time is not linear - it´s a cycle and eventually we will re-member and enter into The Kingdom - to Atlantis - To Heaven once again - bliss - peace - harmony.

As we move along the cycle we realize we are all connected and Love is the glue that holds everything together. By waking up we move away from competition, separation and ego to collaboration, unity and creating from the heart. The new time is to create for the whole just like they do in Damanhur - a Federation of Spiritual Communities located in Italy, north of Piedmont, between Turin and Aosta. In 1975 Falco, Oberto Airaudi (1950-2013) starting realizing his dream by founding Damanhur. He envisioned a fertile reality based on solidarity, sharing, love, and respect for the environment. Approximately 600 citizens live in Damanhur and they give rise to a multilingual society.

According to the vision of these citizens, life is constantly changing and renewed through the relationships and connection with others. It is all about bringing out our truest part which connects us to the divine essence of the universe. This federation of spiritual communities is one example of how we can create for the whole and practice peace and harmony. You can read more about Damanhur on www.damanhur.org.

The pain that we have experienced in the past and which is still ongoing through wars and violence will stop because we have already paid in (pay in = pain). When we wake up we raise our consciousness - we go to a different level of awareness and the outer reality changes. At this level there will be joy and we can appreciate joy since we have experienced pain here in our 3D world. There is no real pain 'there' because we have paid here. We have gone through the experience. That part of the cycle is soon behind us. We never came here to suffer as such, meaning that it was never a choice, who would chose to suffer? It's just that there's simply no way around it.

Waking up is moving on. Re-membering is taking us to a new level of creation, a new level of The Mind where we become more aware of the multidimensional beings we are. We will float into the sea and feel the connection to the whole. Our point of consciousness is no longer separated from 'the rest of the consciousness field.' We start to realize how we are all connected and how unity and collaboration is the way forward. It will help us pull in the same direction to experience peace, harmony and joy for all. We are like cells in a cosmic body. The puzzle is coming together. We help each other by creating and experiencing on a new "level of the game". In this process we continue to define who we really are. Being by doing.

We must move along the cycle and the waking up is part of this cycle. Being stuck in one place would destroy the game. Imagine being stuck in this duality forever with competition, violence and war. We would still be thinking we are our bodies without any reason to be here. It would all be about serving the ego - everyone for him/herself. However, it´s not. We are part of the cycle moving along and we *are* waking up. We had to forget in order to re-member. Consciousness fell when it had 'consumed' all within the finite realm (completed the puzzle). It reached The Paradox Point - the point to infinity - and then it got swiped - consciousness fell and forgot as it had to in order to stay awake and once again re-member. All is Mind and it´s both finite and infinite - The Wake Mind and The Sleeping Mind - His-story (Adam) and Miss Story (mystery - Eve) and as Steve says: This Adam and Eve view is an important one. Why?

Because the paradox sees that there is always two: finite and infinite, male and female, yin and yang, and via understanding we see the struggle for stability and realize that it has to be fluid, it has to keep moving. So symbolically Adam and Eve are our ultimate Father and Mother, and they fell out. We, the children on Earth, come from a broken home due to that fall.

Everything has to join now, science and spirituality, black and white, male and female, rich and poor, strong and weak. We are trying to regain our fluid balance, as Alanis Morissette says:

'We are working our way to our union mended.'

The imbalance we see in the world comes from the fall in the core. You can see the seasons as the ups and downs in a marriage. At the end of the day when all is said and done, there is man and woman and creation comes between.

This book is one of many books about the awakening. I am playing out my character and writing this book as I am supposed to do. It´s part of the cycle like many other tools of awakening: movies, crop circles, The Language of Light, channeled activation images, certain music, energy waves from the cosmos and more. Some people will relate to the content of this book, others might relate to and resonate with crop circles; some will have awakening experiences with channeled information and so on.

You wouldn't be reading this book if you weren't in the process of waking up. You have been drawn to this book for a reason. You are becoming a conscious co-creator. Nothing happens without a reason. As an awakened soul you too can now help re-mind others about Who We Really Are. It's time to realize that you, me and every other soul, every other point of consciousness are the I's of God. We are all *the eyes - I's -* of God. We are God in Disguise. God is *waking up* and moving along the circle and into the next phase - into the Kingdom. You, me and all the rest of us can now create Heaven on Earth because we are becoming *conscious co-creators* creating from the heart for the benefit of *all*.

REFERENCES

1. *Infinity, The Ultimate Trip - Journey Beyond Death.* A Film by Jay Weidner

1.1 World Science Festival - http://worldsciencefestival.com/videos/a_thin_sheet_of_reality_the_universe_as_a_hologram, http://www.youtube.com/watch?v=NsbZT9bJ1s4

2. *I Am That,* Nisargadatta Maharaj, © 2012, The Acorn Press, Durham

3. *The Science of Getting Rich,* Wallace D. Wattles, 1910

4. *The Complete Conversations with God – An Uncommon Dialogue,* Neale Donald Walsh, © 2005, Hampton Roads Publishing Company Inc. and G.P. Putnam's Sons

5. *We Live Forever - The Real Truth About Death,* P.M.H Atwater, © 2004, A.R.E. Press

5.1 The Disappearance of the Universe, Gary R. Renard, Hay House Inc. © 2002, Gary R. Renard

6. *Wikipedia, http://en.wikipedia.org/wiki/Big_Bounce*

7. *The Grand Design,* Stephen Hawking and Leonard Mlodinow, © 2012 - Reprint edition, Bantam

8. *What The Bleep Do We Know? & Down The Rabbit Hole,* DVDs, http://www.whatthebleep.com/index2.shtml

9. *http://www.wired.com/science/discoveries/news/2008/02/qa_turok?currentPage=all*

10. *Consciousness and Beyond - The Final Teachings of Sri Nisargadatta Maharaj,* DVD © Neti Neti Films.

11. *Channeled message from Jeshua through the medium Pamela Kribbe - http://www.jeshua.net*

12. *Channeled message from Bashar through the medium Darryl Anka - http://www.youtube.com/watch?v=om4Nw8VGuh8*

13. *Channeled message from Edgar Cayce - http://www.edgarcayce.org*

14. *http://en.wikipedia.org/wiki/Hermeticism#As_above.2C_so_below*

15. *http://www.deepakchopra.com/blog/view/829/a_consciousness_based_science*

16. *http://wallacewattles.wwwhubs.com/*

17. *Seth Speaks: the Eternal Validity of the Soul,* Jane Roberts and Robert F. Butts (1972), reprinted (1994), Amber-Allen Publishing, p. 41. Reprinted with the permission from New World Library—www.NewWorldLibrary.com

18. *Reincarnation: Born Again and Again,* John Van Auken, © A.R.E. Press (1996)

19. *Think & Grow Rich,* Napoleon Hill, 1937

20. *Darwin's Black Box: The Biochemical Challenge to Evolution,* Michael J. Behe, © Free Press (2006)

21. *The Psychic Energy Codex - Awakening Your Subtle Senses,* Michelle Belanger, © 2007, Red Wheel/Weiser, LLC

22. *Frequency - the Power of Personal Vibration,* Penny Peirce, © 2009, Atria Paperback

23. *The Light Shall Set You* Free, Dr. Norma Milanovich and Dr. Shirley McCune, © 1996, Athena Publishing

24. *Excerpt from The Dore Lectures, Thomas Troward - http:// thomastroward.wwwhubs.com/dore.htm*

25. *The Only Thing That Matters (Conversations with Humanity) - Neal Donald Walsch, © 2012, Emnin Books*

26. *The Symbiotic Universe: Life and mind in the cosmos, George Greenstein, Morrow © 1998,*

27. *The Twelve Layers of DNA - Kryon Book Twelve, Lee Caroll, © 2010, Platinum Publishing House*

28. *Dr. Peter Gajarev - http://www.rexresearch.com/gajarev/ gajarev.htm*

29. *http://near-death.com/experiences/research07.html*

30. *Keys to Soul Evolution - A gateway to the Next Dimension, Jill Mara, © 2009, 7D Publishing and Newsletters from Simion, the 7th dimensional light beings through Jill Mara.*

31. *Bashar - channeled through Darryl Anka: http:// www.youtube.com/watch?v=rcq5tcOzito*

32. *The Masterworks - Explorations in Spiritual Magic, Bryan de*

Flores, www.BryandeFlores.com

33. *Proof of Heaven: A Neurosurgeon's Journey into the Afterlife ,
Eben Alexander,* © *2012 Simon & Schuster - http://
www.thedailybeast.com/newsweek/2012/10/07/proof-of-heaven-a-
doctor-s-experience-with-the-afterlife.html*

34. *Imagining Einstein, Barbara With,* © *2007 Barbara With,
www.barbarawith.com*

35. *The Secret Mind: How your Unconscious Really Shapes your
Decisions. US News and World Report, February 28, 2005*

36. *Dr. Catherine Collautt Ph.D. - http://www.youtube.com/watch?
v=JVJrzLMhyxs*

37. *Spontaneous Evolution - Our positive future, Bruce Lipton PhD
and Steven Bhaerman, Hay House,* © *2011 by Mountain Love
Productions and Steven Bhaerman*

38. *Bob Proctor - http://www.youtube.com/watch?
feature&v=9zkiyaiZFi0*

39. *Wikipedia - http://en.wikipedia.org/wiki/Intuition_
%28psychology%29*

40. *Krishna: The Man and His Philosophy, Osho,* © *1999, South
Asia Books*

41. *Power, Freedom, & Grace: Living from the Source of Lasting
Happiness, Deepak Chopra, Published by Permission of Amber-Allen
Publishing,* © *2006 by Deepak Chopra*

42. *http://www.desikanadadur.com/blog/2009/01/30/free-will-
according-to-sri-nisargadatta-maharaj/*

43. *Napoleon Hill, http://www.youtube.com/watch?
v=UmCtWskzmAQ*

44. *Earl Nightingale - The Strangest Secret - http://www.youtube.com/
watch?v=1Y5g2Pe08uc*

45. *Institute of HeartMath, http://www.heartmath.org/free-services/
articles-of-the-heart/energetic-heart-is-unfolding.html*

46. *http://www.brainyquote.com/quotes/authors/m/
marilyn_ferguson.html*

47. *Kryon Book One, Lee Carrol - 1993, http://www.kryon.com/
k_11.html*

48. *Celestial Voice of Diana - Her Spiritual Guidance to Finding
Love, Rita Eide, Findhorn Pr. © 1999*

49. *David Icke - http://www.theforbiddenknowledge.com/freedom/
index.htm*

50. *Dr. Jill Bolte Taylor - http://www.youtube.com/watch?
&v=UyyjU8fzEYU*

51. *John 14:2 - New International Version, © 1984 - http://bible.cc/
john/14-2.htm*

52. *Transition Now, Redefining Duality, 2012 and Beyond, Martine
Vallée, © 2009. Norwegian copy Cappelen Damm 2011*

53. *Drunvalo* Melchizedek - *http://universalmysteries.co/the-ancient-
secret-of-the-flower-of-life-volume-one-chapter-two/*

54. *The Source Field Investigations, David Wilcock, Penguin Group,*

© 2011

55. *Wikipedia - http://en.wikipedia.org/wiki/Galactic_year*

56. *Pamela Kribb channeling Jeshua http://www.jeshua.net*

57. *Afterlife, A DVD documentary by director Paul Perry, © 2011 Paul Perry Productions*

58. *Excerpt from a letter Voltaire wrote to Frederick William Prince (later King) of Prussia, dated November 28, 1770 - http://www.quotecounterquote.com/2011/02/if-god-did-not-exist-it-would-be.html*

59. *http://www.kryon.com/k_chanelshasta_2_07.html*

60. *http://www.citizenhearing.org/witnesses.html, http://vimeo.com/65430488*

CODES

Hidden within the English language are codes. Few people notice them, but they are there for us to dis-cover - to help us re-member who we really are. Why a Code?

Everything in some way resembles The All as there is nothing else to copy. It is the fractal effect! Therefore, everything is intrinsically encrypted. If you take the word CODE in upper case, turn it upside down, and look at it in the mirror, it still says CODE. It's one of the only words in the English language to do that. It's trying to show that everything is upside-down and back to front.

Mind is all, the physical is the illusion. This 'reflective' CODE then extends into the rest of the English language via multiple meanings of the same word, as in whole and hole. But then you won't spot the CODE if you don't know the cycle, as in real and reel, it means nothing outside the context of the cycle as in that the 'real' is really a reel, a cycle.

In corresponding with Steve Berg I have become aware of many of these codes. I list some of them here for you to see.

ALL ONE = ALONE
Many spiritual people talk about how we are all One, but being All One is being alone. This game is a space-time construct because 'in here' we are not alone (all one). The Mind has created this space-time to experience interaction, being loved and not being alone.

EYES - I's

We are soul aspects of the One and as such we are all the I's - the eyes - of God since we are God in Disguise.

FREE WILL - FREE WHEEL

We are on the cycle of life. The Wheel of life. The river of time appearing to be linear, but going in a cycle ending up where it started. As such we are bound to this wheel and the free will is being free in mind and yet 'trapped' on the forward moving wheel. Like being inside a car on a ride. You are free in mind, but tied to the car moving forward.

GENIUS - GENIE US

We are all genius. We are both logic and magic. The magic is inside us. We all have a Genie inside. Definition of the word genie: A magic spirit believed to take human form and serve the person who calls it. We are God in Disguise.

FINITE - INFINITE

Within the Infinite we find the Finite - the space-time construct created for The Mind to live out its infinite potential. In-Finite

INSIGHT - IN SIGHT

When we quiet the external world we let the **In**ner world bring us sight. **In**-sight.

LIFE - LIE-F

Do you see the lie hiding in the life - Lie-f? This life is an illusion - it is not real even though it feels real. It is a set-up to feel love - to not be alone and as such it is a great set-up. A great gift we must appreciate and honor. Beyond this illusion we are nothing - No Thing. 'In here' we are Some Thing - Every Thing.

MANY - MAN-y

The right brain is our connection to The One, and it speaks to the left brain who is many - the ego - the individual points of consciousness - Man-y. Man is always many. God is One. Man is many. Left brain fools us into thinking we are separate, but in fact we are all One and if we use our right brain and live in the Now we connect with the One.

PAIN = PAY IN

How can we appreciate pleasure if we haven´t endured pain? In our duality/polarity world we experience everything from pain to pleasure. Here we have have to suffer and feel pain. We pay in with pain so we don´t have to pay in on the next stage of the cycle. We pay in with pain 'here' so we don´t have to pay in 'there.' There is no real pain there because we have paid here.

POOL - LOOP

We all come from the same pool (the infinite) and each droplet of this pool can be frozen/defined as a shape/form in the finite space-time construct just as a character in a movie. We come from the same Source, but still we are unique. When we loop back to Source after the experience of finding out Who We Are it´s like we are melting and looping back into the pool - once again joining it after en-riching it with our soul experience. Pool-looP

REAL- REEL

The Mind has to lose it's power in order to be 'real/reel.' We are moving a long a cycle like being part of a movie within the Space-Time Construct. This must be in place in order for The Mind to feel real. It feels *real* when it´s on a *reel*.

RE-MEMBER

By remembering who we are we once again (RE) become a *member* of the Cosmic Mind.

SLEEP - PEELS

Sleep is where we forget to remember. If life is an equation
that unfolds like an onion with many layers/levels, then Sleep
peelS the onion.

SOLE - SOUL purpose

As souls we are here to create and express our uniqueness. We
are here to manifest the un-manifested. This is our sole/soul
purpose.

TIED - TIDE

This shows that we rise and fall. The tide comes in and out.
We don´t stay tied (tie-me) forever. We fall and rise. We forget
to remember who we really are. It´s a cycle.

TIME - TIE-ME

Time ties us down so we can create and experience in the
space-time construct. Tie-Me

TIME - EMIT

Emit is the Big Bang - explosion/implosion/fall in
consciousness and time is the journey back. The linear format
really is a circle looping back on itself.

YOU - U

We really are all 'the same person.' We are not 'one' as in one
big happy family. We are the same Mind out of sync with
itself. Look at the code. We call another 'you.' The word is
'U»…..U-bend……U-turn…It comes right back at U.

TOOLS FOR AWAKENING

This book is one of many tools provided by The Mind to allow us to wake up and re-member who we are. Deep inside there is a longing to move on to the next part of the cycle.

This part involves remembering who we really are - spiritual beings having a physical experience. The longing is becoming stronger and stronger and more tools, like this book, are emerging to help us move along.

Other tools are:

The Universal Laws
Our Universe is run by Universal Laws as real as the laws of physics. Getting to know these laws is getting to know the rules to the Game of Life. You can learn more about these laws by checking out this online course on the teaching platform Udemy:

www.udemy.com/universal-laws .Use this coupon code to receive a nice discount: **theparadox**

The Language of Light
This 'language' (language is in quotes because it cannot be compared with earthly languages the way we perceive language) is of a different order than the phonological language found on Mother Earth.

This universal language is known throughout all of God's creation by all living beings, both physical and non-physical. This is the language of the soul and spirit. It is also called the language of the atoms since every being is fluent in this language on a subconscious level. Our cells react to the frequencies in this language. People report that they feel at home when listening to it.

You can read more about this language in my first book *The Shift in Consciousness* (www.TheShiftInConsciousness.com).

You can also see videos, download mp3s, PDFs and read more about the language on the website I have created for the book and the language here:

http://www.theshiftinconsciousness.com/the-language-of-light

Spiritual movies
The last 10-15 years we have seen a wide range of spiritual movies and documentaries emerge. Movies like Powder, Way of The Peaceful Warrior, What The Bleep Do We Know?, The Celestine Prophecy, Infinity - The Ultimate Trip, The Day Before Disclosure, Avatar and many more.

These movies and others like them touch the essence of who we really are. They touch the soul within. They are tools to help us re-member.

I have collected several free online spiritual movies on my website CamilloLoken.com/en

You can check them out using this shortened URL taking you to Free Spiritual Movies: http://bit.ly/12ruH57

Books
This book contains many references to other books which might be of help in this awakening process. These books,

along with other tools, have helped me expand my consciousness. Maybe they might do the same for you. Check out the list of books in the Reference list.

Accelerators by Bryan de Flores

I teamed up with Bryan de Flores after he had read my first book The Shift in Consciousness in the summer of 2012. He invited me over to the US to speak at his spiritual conferences in Mount Shasta, California and Sedona, Arizona. At these conferences I became familiar with his channeled images/ accelerators from The Ashtar Command.

These images contain sacred geometry, mathematical configurations and light frequencies that will help us wake up and re-member who we are.

Since his own awakening in 2006 Bryan has drawn 13.000 images and each of them is completed in a matter of minutes (5 – 15 minutes).

If you are located in Scandinavia you can read more about these incredible drawings/accelerators on my Norwegian website here:
www.camilloloken.com/selvutvikling/aktiveringsbilder

You can also check out Bryan's English website with the accelerators here: www.bryandeflores.com

Crop Circles

Crop circles are also containing symbols and energies helping us re-member. In the summer of 2011 my family and myself enjoyed visiting many crop circles in the UK. A very interesting experience.

There are many great websites featuring the latest updates on crop circles in the UK and elsewhere. My good friend Terje Toftenes and his filmteam have made a great documentary on crop circles.

See the full documentary here: http://www.youtube.com/watch?v=qtUZBwTvOV8

You can also buy the DVD from his website here: http://newparadigmfilms.squarespace.com/our-films

FREE E-BOOKS AND AUDIO

Free e-books

During my search for answers to who we are and why we are here I came across some great books written many years ago by Wallace D. Watteles, Napoleon Hill and Charles F. Haanel.

These are:

The Science of Getting Rich by Wallace D. Wattles
The Master Key System by Charles F. Haanel
Think & Grow Rich by Napoleon Hill

You can now read their words of wisdom through the free e-book service I offer on one of my websites: One Mind - One Energy.

Gain access here:
http://www.one-mind-one-energy.com/ebooks.html

Free audio

You can also gain access to a great audio recording done by Earl Nightingale in 1956 called **The Strangest Secret**. It contains great words of wisdom. Access it from my website: http://www.one-mind-one-energy.com/Freestuff.html (Scroll down on the site to access it)

Camillo´s websites, Twitter, YouTube & Facebook

Websites:
www.CamilloLoken.com/en
www.WakeUpURGod.com
www.one-mind-one-energy.com
www.TheShiftinConsciousness.com

Twitter, YouTube & Facebook:
twitter.com/1Mind1Energy
www.youtube.com/1Mind1Energy
www.facebook.com/Camillo8

Printed in Great Britain
by Amazon

73993688R00161